# Quick & Easy
# Healthy Eating

*p*

# Contents

Introduction . . . . . . . . . . . . . . . . . . . . . . . . . . . .4

Chicken & Leek Soup . . . . . . . . . . . . . . . . . . . . . . .6

Beef Soup with Rice . . . . . . . . . . . . . . . . . . . . . . . .7

Minted Onion Bhajis . . . . . . . . . . . . . . . . . . . . . . .8

Vegetables with Tahini Dip . . . . . . . . . . . . . . . . . .9

Bruschetta . . . . . . . . . . . . . . . . . . . . . . . . . . . . . .10

Cheesy Ham Savoury . . . . . . . . . . . . . . . . . . . . . .11

Spicy Chickpea Snack . . . . . . . . . . . . . . . . . . . . .12

Crêpes with Curried Crab . . . . . . . . . . . . . . . . . .13

Cranberry turkey Burgers . . . . . . . . . . . . . . . . . .14

Stuffed Mushrooms . . . . . . . . . . . . . . . . . . . . . . .15

Pasta Provençale . . . . . . . . . . . . . . . . . . . . . . . . .16

Lamb & Tomato Koftas . . . . . . . . . . . . . . . . . . . .17

Cheese & Chive Scones . . . . . . . . . . . . . . . . . . . .18

Oat-Crusted Chicken Pieces . . . . . . . . . . . . . . . .19

Hot Pot Chops . . . . . . . . . . . . . . . . . . . . . . . . . .20

Kibbeh . . . . . . . . . . . . . . . . . . . . . . . . . . . . . . . .21

Lamb with a Spice Crust . . . . . . . . . . . . . . . . . . .22

Pork & Apple Skewers . . . . . . . . . . . . . . . . . . . . .23

Ginger Beef with Chilli . . . . . . . . . . . . . . . . . . . .24

Meatball Brochettes . . . . . . . . . . . . . . . . . . . . . .25

Pork with Ratatouille Sauce . . . . . . . . . . . . . . . .26

Sweet Lamb Fillet . . . . . . . . . . . . . . . . . . . . . . . .27

Tangy Pork Fillet . . . . . . . . . . . . . . . . . . . . . . . . .28

Teppanyaki . . . . . . . . . . . . . . . . . . . . . . . . . . . . .29

Karahi Chicken . . . . . . . . . . . . . . . . . . . . . . . . . .30

Lime Chicken Kebabs . . . . . . . . . . . . . . . . . . . . .31

Cajun Chicken Gumbo . . . . . . . . . . . . . . . . . . . . . . . . . .32

Citrus Duckling Skewers . . . . . . . . . . . . . . . . . . . . . . .33

Ginger Chicken & Corn . . . . . . . . . . . . . . . . . . . . . . . .34

Mexican Chicken . . . . . . . . . . . . . . . . . . . . . . . . . . . .35

Prawn Bhuna . . . . . . . . . . . . . . . . . . . . . . . . . . . . . . . .36

Salmon Yakitori . . . . . . . . . . . . . . . . . . . . . . . . . . . . . .37

Baked Sea Bass . . . . . . . . . . . . . . . . . . . . . . . . . . . . . .38

Curried Crab . . . . . . . . . . . . . . . . . . . . . . . . . . . . . . . .39

Lemony Monkfish Skewers . . . . . . . . . . . . . . . . . . . . .40

Fragrant Tuna Steaks . . . . . . . . . . . . . . . . . . . . . . . . .41

Char-Grilled Mackerel . . . . . . . . . . . . . . . . . . . . . . . .42

Scallop Skewers . . . . . . . . . . . . . . . . . . . . . . . . . . . . .43

Green Fish Curry . . . . . . . . . . . . . . . . . . . . . . . . . . . . .44

Plaice with Mushrooms . . . . . . . . . . . . . . . . . . . . . . . .45

Fish with Black Bean Sauce . . . . . . . . . . . . . . . . . . . .46

Scallops with Mushrooms . . . . . . . . . . . . . . . . . . . . . .47

Baked Trout Mexican-Style . . . . . . . . . . . . . . . . . . . .48

Oriental Vegetable Noodles . . . . . . . . . . . . . . . . . . . .49

Char-Grilled Vegetables . . . . . . . . . . . . . . . . . . . . . . .50

Spinach & Orange Salad . . . . . . . . . . . . . . . . . . . . . .51

Coronation Salad . . . . . . . . . . . . . . . . . . . . . . . . . . . .52

Minted Fennel Salad . . . . . . . . . . . . . . . . . . . . . . . . .53

Moroccan Couscous Salad . . . . . . . . . . . . . . . . . . . . .54

Mussel Salad . . . . . . . . . . . . . . . . . . . . . . . . . . . . . . .55

Sweet & Sour Fruit . . . . . . . . . . . . . . . . . . . . . . . . . .56

Carrot & Orange Salad . . . . . . . . . . . . . . . . . . . . . . .57

Tomato Salsa . . . . . . . . . . . . . . . . . . . . . . . . . . . . . . .58

Aubergine Curry . . . . . . . . . . . . . . . . . . . . . . . . . . . . .59

Sesame Seed Chutney . . . . . . . . . . . . . . . . . . . . . . . .60

Colcannon . . . . . . . . . . . . . . . . . . . . . . . . . . . . . . . . . .61

Chocolate & Pineapple Cake . . . . . . . . . . . . . . . . . . .62

Tropical Fruit Fool . . . . . . . . . . . . . . . . . . . . . . . . . . .63

# Introduction

**Healthy eating means that you can enjoy all of your favourite foods and still keep in great shape. These carefully selected recipes will show you how you can eat nutritious, filling, well-balanced meals, full of flavour and low in fat. Packed full of dishes that are quick and simple to prepare, *Low Fat* provides an array of healthy, low-fat dishes for you, your family and your guests to enjoy.**

## Reducing Your Fat Intake

Reducing the fat content in our diet is very easy, and the benefits are myriad. Not only do supermarkets provide a variety of healthy alternatives to full-fat ingredients, such as reduced-fat dairy products, but the variety of fresh fruit and vegetables available provides excellent sources of essential vitamins. The easiest and quickest way to reduce your fat calorie intake is to change from full-fat milk, cream, cheese and yoghurt to a low- or reduced-fat equivalent. Semi-skimmed milk, for example, has all the nutritional benefits of whole milk but 10 g/$^1$/$_3$ oz of fat per pint compared with 23 g/$^3$/$_4$ oz of fat per pint in whole milk.

## The Benefits of Fat

Reducing the level of fat in your diet is synonymous with losing weight. Yet there are many benefits in eating the right types of fat of which many dieters are unaware. It is important to remember that we all need to include a certain amount of fat in our daily intake to function properly. Essential fatty acids are required in order to build cell membranes and for other vital bodily functions. Our brain tissues, nerve sheaths and bone marrow need fat, and we also need fat to protect our organs such as our liver, kidneys and heart.

## When is Fat Bad?

Fat is bad when we consume a high level of it in our diet. Too much fat increases the risk of developing coronary disease, diabetes and even cancer — and, of course, it can lead to obesity. But high-fat diet-related illnesses are not limited to those who are overweight.

Nutritionists suggest that we should aim to cut our intake of fat to 27—30 per cent of our total daily calorie intake. If your average diet totals 2000 calories, this will mean eating no more than about 75 g/2$^3$/$_4$ oz of fat a day. As a guide, most people consume 40 per cent of their daily calories in the form of fat. However, you should always consult your family doctor if you are being treated for any medical condition before you begin a new regime.

## Different Types of Fat

Fats are made up of a combination of fatty acids and glycerol. Fatty acids consist of a chain of carbon atoms linked to hydrogen atoms. The way these are linked determines whether they are saturated or unsaturated fats, and consequently if they should be avoided or not.

Saturated fats. These are easily recognisable. Saturated fats are solid at room temperature and are mainly found in animal products, such as meat and dairy foods, although some vegetable oils, including palm and coconut oil, contain them.

Our body has difficulty processing these saturated fats and, as a result, it tends to store them. They increase cholesterol levels in the bloodstream, which can in turn increase the risk of heart disease. It is therefore important to reduce the level of saturated fats in the diet: they should comprise no more than 30 per cent of the total fat intake or no more than nine per cent of the total energy intake.

Unsaturated fats. These are normally liquid or soft at room temperature and are thought to reduce the level of cholesterol in the bloodstream. There are two types of unsaturated fats: monounsaturated and polyunsaturated. The former are mainly found in vegetables, but they also occur in oily fish, such as mackerel. The latter are only found in oily fish and seed oils.

## Cooking Methods

The way we cook our food is one of the most important factors in ensuring a healthy, low-fat diet. In general, steaming is the best way to cook vegetables to preserve their goodness. Boiling can, for example, destroy up to three-quarters of the vitamin C present in green vegetables. This guide will help you to choose the healthiest way to cook your dish, while maintaining optimum flavour and colour.

| KEY |
| --- |
| 🍞 Simplicity level 1 – 3 (1 easiest, 3 slightly harder) |
| 🥗 Preparation time |
| 🕐 Cooking time |

- **Frying**. This is the most fat-rich method of cooking. Yet, surprisingly, deep-frying the food absorbs less fat than shallow-frying. To cut down on fat intake, buy a good quality, non-stick frying pan as you will need less fat, and use a vegetable oil, high in polyunsaturates. A good method is to stir-fry food: you require little oil as the food is cooked quickly over a high heat.

- **Grilling**. This is a good alternative to frying, producing a crisp, golden coating whilst keeping food tender and moist. Ingredients with a delicate texture and which can easily dry out, such as white fish or chicken breasts, will require brushing with oil. Marinating can reduce the need for oil. Always cook on a rack, so that the fat drains away.

- **Poaching**. This is ideal for foods with a delicate texture or subtle flavour, such as chicken and fish, and it is fat free. The cooking liquid can make the basis of a nutritious and flavoursome sauce: try alternative liquids such as stock, wine and acidulated water, flavoured with herbs and vegetables.

- **Steaming**. This is also fat-free and is becoming a popular method of cooking meat, fish, chicken and vegetables. Ingredients maintain their colour, flavour and texture, fewer nutrients are leached out. An additional advantage is that when meat is steamed, the fat melts and drips into the cooking liquid – this should not then be used for gravy.

- **Braising and stewing**. Slow-cooking techniques produce succulent dishes that are especially welcome in winter. Trim all visible fat from the meat and always remove the skin from the chicken.

- **Roasting**. Fat is an integral part of this cooking technique and without it meat or fish would dry out. Try standing meat on a rack over a roasting tray so that the fat drains off. Do not use the meat juices for gravy.

- **Baking**. Many dishes are fat free. Foil-wrapped parcels of meat or fish are always delicious. Add fruit juice or wine instead of oil or butter for a moist texture.

- **Microwave**. Food cooked in this way rarely requires additional fat.

# Chicken & Leek Soup

This satisfying soup can be served as a main course. You can add rice and peppers to make it even more hearty, as well as colourful.

## NUTRITIONAL INFORMATION

| | | | |
|---|---|---|---|
| Calories | .......183 | Sugar | .........4g |
| Protein | ........21g | Fats | ...........9g |
| Carbohydrates | ....4g | Saturates | ......5g |

5 MINS     1¼ HOURS

### SERVES 4–6

## INGREDIENTS

25 g/1 oz/2 tbsp butter

350 g/12 oz boneless chicken

350 g/12 oz leeks, cut into 2.5-cm/
   1-inch pieces

1.2 litres/2 pints chicken stock

1 bouquet garni sachet

8 pitted prunes, halved

salt and white pepper

cooked rice and diced peppers (optional)

1 Melt the butter in a large saucepan.

2 Add the chicken and leeks to the saucepan and fry for 8 minutes.

3 Add the chicken stock and bouquet garni sachet and stir well.

4 Season well with salt and pepper to taste.

5 Bring the soup to the boil and simmer for 45 minutes.

6 Add the prunes to the saucepan with some cooked rice and diced peppers (if using) and simmer for about 20 minutes.

7 Remove the bouquet garni sachet from the soup and discard. Serve the chicken and leek soup immediately.

## VARIATION

Instead of the bouquet garni sachet, you can use a bunch of fresh mixed herbs, tied together with string. Choose herbs such as parsley, thyme and rosemary.

# Beef Soup with Rice

Strips of tender lean beef are combined with crisp water chestnuts and cooked rice in a tasty beef broth with a tang of orange.

## NUTRITIONAL INFORMATION

| | | |
|---|---|---|
| Calories . . . . . . . .210 | Sugar . . . . . . . . .4g |
| Protein . . . . . . . .20g | Fats . . . . . . . . . . .5g |
| Carbohydrates . . .21g | Saturates . . . . . .2g |

25 MINS         25 MINS

### SERVES 4

## INGREDIENTS

350 g/12 oz lean beef (such as rump or sirloin)

1 litre/1¾ pints beef stock

1 cinnamon stick, broken

2 star anise

2 tbsp dark soy sauce

2 tbsp dry sherry

3 tbsp tomato purée

115 g/4 oz can water chestnuts, drained and sliced

175 g/6 oz cooked white rice

1 tsp zested orange rind

6 tbsp orange juice

salt and pepper

### TO GARNISH

strips of orange rind

2 tbsp chives, snipped

1 Carefully trim away any fat from the beef. Cut the beef into thin strips and then place into a large saucepan.

2 Pour over the stock and add the cinnamon, star anise, soy sauce, sherry, tomato purée and water chestnuts. Bring to the boil, skimming away any surface scum with a flat ladle. Cover the pan and simmer gently for about 20 minutes.

3 Skim the soup with a flat ladle to remove any more scum. Remove and discard the cinnamon and star anise and blot the surface with absorbent kitchen paper to remove any fat.

4 Stir in the rice, orange rind and juice. Check the seasoning. Heat through for 2–3 minutes before ladling into warm bowls. Serve garnished with strips of orange rind and snipped chives.

### COOK'S TIP

Omit the rice for a lighter soup that is an ideal starter for an Oriental meal of many courses. For a more substantial soup that would be a meal in its own right, add diced vegetables such as carrot, pepper, sweetcorn or courgette.

# Minted Onion Bhajis

Gram flour (also known as besan flour) is a fine yellow flour made from chickpeas and is available from supermarkets and Asian food shops.

## NUTRITIONAL INFORMATION

| | | |
|---|---|---|
| Calories | . . . . . . . .251 | Sugars . . . . . . . . .7g |
| Protein | . . . . . . . . .7g | Fat . . . . . . . . . . .8g |
| Carbohydrate | . . .39g | Saturates . . . . . .1g |

5 MINS          15 MINS

### MAKES 12

## I N G R E D I E N T S

125 g/4½ oz gram flour

¼ tsp cayenne pepper

¼–½ tsp ground coriander

¼–½ tsp ground cumin

1 tbsp chopped fresh mint

4 tbsp strained thick low-fat yogurt

65 ml/2½ fl oz cold water

1 large onion, quartered and thinly sliced

vegetable oil, for frying

salt and pepper

sprigs of mint, to garnish

1 Put the gram flour into a bowl, add the cayenne pepper, coriander, cumin and mint and season with salt and pepper to taste. Stir in the yogurt, water and sliced onion and mix well together.

2 One-third fill a large, deep frying pan with oil and heat until very hot. Drop heaped spoonfuls of the mixture, a few at a time, into the hot oil and use two forks to neaten the mixture into rough ball-shapes.

3 Fry the bhajis until golden brown and cooked through, turning frequently.

4 Drain the bhajis on absorbent kitchen paper (paper towels) and keep warm while cooking the remainder in the same way.

5 Arrange the bhajis on a platter and garnish with sprigs of fresh mint. Serve hot or warm.

## COOK'S TIP

Gram flour is excellent for making batter and is used in India in place of flour. It can be made from ground split peas as well as chickpeas.

# Vegetables with Tahini Dip

This tasty dip is great for livening-up simply-cooked vegetables.
You can vary the vegetables according to the season.

## NUTRITIONAL INFORMATION

| | | |
|---|---|---|
| Calories ........126 | Sugars .........7g | |
| Protein .........11g | Fat ...........6g | |
| Carbohydrate ....8g | Saturates ......1g | |

5 MINS          20 MINS

### SERVES 4

## INGREDIENTS

225 g/8 oz small broccoli florets

225 g/8 oz small cauliflower florets

225 g/8 oz asparagus, sliced into 5 cm/
 2 inch lengths

2 small red onions, quartered

1 tbsp lime juice

2 tsp toasted sesame seeds

1 tbsp chopped fresh chives, to garnish

### HOT TAHINI & GARLIC DIP

1 tsp sunflower oil

2 garlic cloves, crushed

½–1 tsp chilli powder

2 tsp tahini (sesame seed paste)

150 ml/¼ pint low-fat natural fromage frais

2 tbsp chopped fresh chives

salt and pepper

1 Line the base of a steamer with baking parchment and arrange the vegetables on top.

2 Bring a wok or large saucepan of water to the boil, and place the steamer on top. Sprinkle with lime juice and steam for 10 minutes.

3 To make the hot tahini & garlic dip, heat the sunflower oil in a small non-stick saucepan, add the garlic, chilli powder and seasoning to taste and fry gently for 2–3 minutes until the garlic is softened.

4 Remove the saucepan from the heat and stir in the tahini (sesame seed paste) and fromage frais. Return to the heat and cook gently for 1–2 minutes without boiling. Stir in the chives.

5 Remove the vegetables from the steamer and place on a warmed serving platter. Sprinkle with the sesame seeds and garnish with chopped chives. Serve with the hot dip.

# Bruschetta

Traditionally, this Italian savoury is enriched with olive oil. Here, sun-dried tomatoes are a good substitute and only a little oil is used.

## NUTRITIONAL INFORMATION

| | | |
|---|---|---|
| Calories .......178 | Sugars .........2g | |
| Protein .........8g | Fat ..........6g | |
| Carbohydrate ...24g | Saturates ......2g | |

45 MINS     5 MINS

### SERVES 4

## INGREDIENTS

60 g/2 oz dry-pack sun-dried tomatoes

300 ml/½ pint boiling water

35 cm/14 inch long Granary or wholemeal stick of French bread

1 large garlic clove, halved

25 g/1 oz pitted black olives in brine, drained and quartered

2 tsp olive oil

2 tbsp chopped fresh basil

40 g/1½ oz grated low-fat Italian Mozzarella cheese

salt and pepper

fresh basil leaves, to garnish

1 Place the sun-dried tomatoes in a heatproof bowl and pour over the boiling water.

2 Set aside for 30 minutes to soften. Drain well and pat dry with paper towels. Slice into thin strips and set aside.

3 Trim and discard the ends from the bread and cut into 12 slices. Arrange on a grill rack and place under a preheated hot grill and cook for 1–2 minutes on each side until lightly golden.

4 Rub both sides of each piece of bread with the cut sides of the garlic. Top with strips of sun-dried tomato and olives.

5 Brush lightly with olive oil and season well. Sprinkle with the basil and Mozzarella cheese and return to the grill for 1–2 minutes until the cheese is melted and bubbling.

6 Transfer to a warmed serving platter and garnish with fresh basil leaves.

## COOK'S TIP

If you use sun-dried tomatoes packed in oil, drain them, rinse well in warm water and drain again on kitchen paper (paper towels) to remove as much oil as possible. Sun-dried tomatoes give a rich, full flavour to this dish, but thinly-sliced fresh tomatoes can be used instead.

# Cheesy Ham Savoury

Lean ham wrapped around crisp celery, topped with a light crust of cheese and spring onions, makes a delicious light lunch.

## NUTRITIONAL INFORMATION

| | | |
|---|---|---|
| Calories .......188 | Sugars .........5g | |
| Protein ........15g | Fat ..........12g | |
| Carbohydrate ....5g | Saturates ......7g | |

🥧 10 MINS    🕐 10 MINS

### SERVES 4

## I N G R E D I E N T S

4 sticks celery, with leaves

12 thin slices of lean ham

1 bunch spring onions

175 g/6 oz low-fat soft cheese with garlic and herbs

6 tbsp low-fat natural yogurt

4 tbsp Parmesan cheese, freshly grated

celery salt and pepper

### T O   S E R V E

tomato salad

crusty bread

1 Wash the celery, remove the leaves and reserve (if wished). Slice each celery stick into 3 equal portions.

2 Cut any visible fat off the ham and lay the slices on a chopping board. Place a piece of celery on each piece of ham and roll up. Place 3 ham and celery rolls in each of 4 small, heatproof dishes.

3 Trim the spring onions, then finely shred both the white and green parts. Sprinkle the spring onions over the ham and celery rolls and season with celery salt and pepper.

4 Mix the soft cheese and yogurt and spoon over the ham and celery rolls.

5 Preheat the grill to medium. Sprinkle each portion with 1 tbsp grated Parmesan cheese and grill for 6–7 minutes until hot and the cheese has formed a crust. If the cheese starts to brown too quickly, lower the grill setting slightly.

6 Garnish with celery leaves (if using) and serve with a tomato salad and crusty bread.

### COOK'S TIP

Parmesan is useful in low-fat recipes because its intense flavour means you need to use only a small amount.

# Spicy Chickpea Snack

You can use fresh chickpeas, soaked overnight, for this popular Indian snack, but the canned variety is just as flavoursome.

## NUTRITIONAL INFORMATION

| | |
|---|---|
| Calories .......190 | Sugars .........4g |
| Protein .........9g | Fat ...........3g |
| Carbohydrate ...34g | Saturates .....0.3g |

5 MINS     10 MINS

### SERVES 4

## I N G R E D I E N T S

400 g/14 oz can chickpeas, drained

2 medium potatoes

1 medium onion

2 tbsp tamarind paste

6 tbsp water

1 tsp chilli powder

2 tsp sugar

1 tsp salt

### T O   G A R N I S H

1 tomato, sliced

2 fresh green chillies, chopped

fresh coriander leaves

1 Place the chickpeas in a bowl.

## COOK'S TIP

Chickpeas have a nutty flavour and slightly crunchy texture. Indian cooks also grind these to make a flour called gram or besan, which is used to make breads, thicken sauces, and to make batters for deep-fried dishes.

2 Using a sharp knife, cut the potatoes into dice.

3 Place the potatoes in a saucepan of water and boil until cooked through. Test by inserting the tip of a knife into the potatoes – they should feel soft and tender. Set the potatoes aside.

4 Using a sharp knife, finely chop the onion. Set aside until required.

5 Mix together the tamarind paste and water. Add the chilli powder, sugar and salt and mix again. Pour the mixture over the chickpeas.

6 Add the onion and the diced potatoes, and stir to mix. Season to taste.

7 Transfer to a serving bowl and garnish with tomatoes, chillies and coriander leaves.

# Crêpes with Curried Crab

Home-made crêpes are delicious – here, white crab meat is lightly flavoured with curry spices and tossed in a low-fat dressing.

## NUTRITIONAL INFORMATION

| | |
|---|---|
| Calories .......279 | Sugars .........9g |
| Protein ........25g | Fat ...........7g |
| Carbohydrate ...31g | Saturates ......1g |

🕑 40 MINS    🕐 25 MINS

### SERVES 4

## I N G R E D I E N T S

115 g/4 oz buckwheat flour

1 large egg, beaten

300 ml/½ pint skimmed milk

125 g/4½ oz frozen spinach, thawed, well-drained and chopped

2 tsp vegetable oil

### F I L L I N G

350 g/12 oz white crab meat

1 tsp mild curry powder

1 tbsp mango chutney

1 tbsp reduced-calorie mayonnaise

2 tbsp low-fat natural yogurt

2 tbsp fresh coriander, chopped

### T O  S E R V E

green salad

lemon wedges

1 Sift the flour into a bowl and remove any husks that remain in the sieve. Make a well in the centre of the flour and add the egg. Whisk in the milk, then blend in the spinach. Transfer to a jug and leave for 30 minutes.

2 To make the filling, mix together all the ingredients, except the coriander, in a bowl, cover and chill until required. Whisk the batter. Brush a small crêpe pan with a little oil, heat until hot and pour in enough batter to cover the base thinly. Cook for 1–2 minutes, turn over and cook for 1 minute until golden. Repeat to make 8 pancakes, layering them on a plate with baking parchment.

3 Stir the coriander into the crab mixture. Fold each pancake into quarters. Open one fold and fill with the crab mixture. Serve warm, with a green salad and lemon wedges.

### VARIATION

Try lean diced chicken in a light white sauce or peeled prawns instead of the crab.

# Cranberry Turkey Burgers

This recipe is bound to be popular with children and is easy to prepare for their supper or tea.

## NUTRITIONAL INFORMATION

| | |
|---|---|
| Calories .......209 | Sugars ........15g |
| Protein ........22g | Fat ..........5g |
| Carbohydrate ...21g | Saturates ......1g |

🐾 🐾

🍖 45 MINS     🕐 25 MINS

### SERVES 4

## I N G R E D I E N T S

350 g/12 oz lean minced turkey

1 onion, chopped finely

1 tbsp chopped fresh sage

6 tbsp dry white breadcrumbs

4 tbsp cranberry sauce

1 egg white, size 2, lightly beaten

2 tsp sunflower oil

salt and pepper

### TO SERVE

4 toasted granary or wholemeal
　burger buns

½ lettuce, shredded

4 tomatoes, sliced

4 tsp cranberry sauce

1 Mix together the turkey, onion, sage, seasoning, breadcrumbs and cranberry sauce, then bind with egg white.

2 Press into 4 x 10 cm/4 inch rounds, about 2 cm/¾ inch thick. Chill the burgers for 30 minutes.

3 Line a grill rack with baking parchment, making sure the ends are secured underneath the rack to ensure they don't catch fire. Place the burgers on top and brush lightly with oil. Put under a preheated moderate grill and cook for 10 minutes. Turn the burgers over, brush again with oil. Cook for a further 12–15 minutes until cooked through.

4 Fill the burger rolls with lettuce, tomato and a burger, and top with cranberry sauce.

## COOK'S TIP

Look out for a variety of ready minced meats at your butchers or supermarket. If unavailable, you can mince your own by choosing lean cuts and processing them in a blender or food processor.

# Stuffed Mushrooms

Large mushrooms have more flavour than the smaller button mushrooms. Serve these mushrooms as a side vegetable or appetizer.

## NUTRITIONAL INFORMATION

| | | |
|---|---|---|
| Calories .......148 | Sugars .........1g | |
| Protein ........11g | Fat ...........7g | |
| Carbohydrate ....11g | Saturates ......3g | |

🔶 🔶

🍲 10 MINS     🕐 15 MINS

**SERVES 4**

## I N G R E D I E N T S

12 open-cap mushrooms

4 spring onions, chopped

4 tsp olive oil

100 g/3½ oz fresh brown breadcrumbs

1 tsp fresh oregano, chopped

100 g/3½ oz low-fat mature
    Cheddar cheese

1 Wash the mushrooms and pat dry with kitchen paper. Remove the stalks and chop the stalks finely.

2 Sauté the mushroom stalks and spring onions in half of the oil.

3 In a large bowl, mix together the mushroom stalks and spring onions.

4 Add the breadcrumbs and oregano to the mushrooms and spring onions, mix and set aside.

5 Crumble the cheese into small pieces in a small bowl. Add the cheese to the breadcrumb mixture and mix well. Spoon the stuffing mixture into the mushroom caps.

6 Drizzle the remaining oil over the mushrooms. Barbecue on an oiled rack over medium hot coals for 10 minutes or until cooked through.

7 Transfer the mushrooms to serving plates and serve hot.

## VARIATION

For a change replace the cheese with finely-chopped chorizo sausage (remove the skin first), chopped hard-boiled eggs, chopped olives or chopped anchovy fillets. Mop up the juices with some crusty bread.

# Pasta Provençale

A combination of Italian vegetables tossed in a tomato dressing, served on a bed of assorted salad leaves, makes an appetizing meal.

## NUTRITIONAL INFORMATION

| | | | |
|---|---|---|---|
| Calories | .......197 | Sugars | .........5g |
| Protein | ........10g | Fat | ...........5g |
| Carbohydrate | ...30g | Saturates | ......1g |

10 MINS     15 MINS

### SERVES 4

## INGREDIENTS

225 g/8 oz penne

1 tbsp olive oil

25 g/1 oz pitted black olives, drained and chopped

25 g/1 oz dry-pack sun-dried tomatoes, soaked, drained and chopped

400 g/14 oz can artichoke hearts, drained and halved

115 g/4 oz baby courgettes, trimmed and sliced

115 g/4 oz baby plum tomatoes, halved

100 g/3½ oz assorted baby salad leaves

salt and pepper

shredded basil leaves, to garnish

## DRESSING

4 tbsp passata

2 tbsp low-fat natural fromage frais

1 tbsp unsweetened orange juice

1 small bunch fresh basil, shredded

1 Cook the penne according to the instructions on the packet. Do not overcook the pasta – it should still have 'bite'. Drain well and return to the pan.

2 Stir in the olive oil, salt and pepper, olives and sun-dried tomatoes. Leave to cool.

3 Gently mix the artichokes, courgettes and plum tomatoes into the cooked pasta. Arrange the salad leaves in a serving bowl.

4 To make the dressing, mix all the ingredients together and toss into the vegetables and pasta.

5 Spoon the mixture on top of the salad leaves and garnish with shredded basil leaves.

# Lamb & Tomato Koftas

These little meatballs, served with a minty yogurt dressing, can be prepared well in advance, ready to cook when required.

## NUTRITIONAL INFORMATION

Calories . . . . . . .183   Sugars . . . . . . . . .5g
Protein . . . . . . . .15g   Fat . . . . . . . . . . .11g
Carbohydrate . . . .5g   Saturates . . . . . .4g

15 MINS          10 MINS

### SERVES 4

## I N G R E D I E N T S

225 g/8 oz finely minced lean lamb

1½ onions, peeled

1-2 garlic cloves, peeled and crushed

1 dried red chilli, finely chopped (optional)

2-3 tsp garam masala

2 tbsp chopped fresh mint

2 tsp lemon juice

salt

2 tbsp vegetable oil

4 small tomatoes, quartered

mint sprigs, to garnish

## Y O G U R T   D R E S S I N G

150 ml/¼ pint low-fat yogurt

5 cm/2 inch piece cucumber, grated

2 tbsp chopped fresh mint

½ tsp toasted cumin seeds (optional)

1 Place the minced lamb in a bowl. Finely chop 1 onion and add to the bowl with the garlic and chilli (if using). Stir in the garam masala, mint and lemon juice and season well with salt. Mix well.

2 Divide the mixture in half, then divide each half into 10 equal portions and form each into a small ball. Roll balls in the oil to coat. Quarter the remaining onion half and separate into layers.

3 Thread 5 of the spicy meatballs, 4 tomato quarters and some of the onion layers on to each of 4 pre-soaked bamboo or metal skewers.

4 Brush the vegetables with the remaining oil and cook the koftas under a hot grill for about 10 minutes, turning frequently until they are browned all over and cooked through.

5 Meanwhile, prepare the yogurt dressing for the koftas. In a small bowl mix together the yogurt, grated cucumber, mint and toasted cumin seeds (if using).

6 Garnish the lamb and tomato koftas with mint sprigs and place on a large serving platter. Serve the koftas hot with the yogurt dressing.

# Cheese & Chive Scones

These tea-time classics have been given a healthy twist by the use of low-fat soft cheese and reduced-fat Cheddar cheese.

## NUTRITIONAL INFORMATION

| | |
|---|---|
| Calories .......297 | Sugars .........3g |
| Protein ........13g | Fat ...........7g |
| Carbohydrate ...49g | Saturates ......4g |

🌰 🌰

🥘 10 MINS   🕐 20 MINS

### MAKES 10

## INGREDIENTS

225 g/8 oz self-raising flour

1 tsp powdered mustard

½ tsp cayenne pepper

½ tsp salt

100 g/3½ oz low-fat soft cheese with added herbs

2 tbsp fresh snipped chives, plus extra to garnish

100 ml/3½ fl oz and 2 tbsp skimmed milk

60 g/2 oz reduced-fat mature Cheddar cheese, grated

low-fat soft cheese, to serve

1 Preheat the oven to 200°C/400°F/Gas Mark 6. Sift the flour, mustard, cayenne and salt into a mixing bowl.

2 Add the soft cheese to the mixture and mix together until well incorporated. Stir in the snipped chives.

3 Make a well in the centre of the ingredients and gradually pour in 100 ml/3½ fl oz milk, stirring as you pour, until the mixture forms a soft dough.

4 Turn the dough on to a floured surface and knead lightly. Roll out until 2 cm/¾ inch thick and use a 5 cm/2 inch plain pastry cutter to stamp out as many rounds as you can. Transfer the rounds to a baking sheet.

5 Re-knead the dough trimmings together and roll out again. Stamp out more rounds – you should be able to make 10 scones in total.

6 Brush the scones with the remaining milk and sprinkle with the grated cheese. Bake in the oven for 15–20 minutes until risen and golden. Transfer to a wire rack to cool. Serve warm with low-fat soft cheese, garnished with chives.

## VARIATION

For sweet scones, omit the mustard, cayenne pepper, chives and grated cheese. Replace the flavoured soft cheese with plain low-fat soft cheese. Add 75 g/2¾ oz currants and 25 g/ 1 oz caster sugar. Serve with low-fat soft cheese and fruit spread.

# Oat-Crusted Chicken Pieces

A very low-fat chicken recipe with a refreshingly light, mustard-spiced sauce, which is ideal for a healthy lunchbox or a light meal with salad.

## NUTRITIONAL INFORMATION

| | | |
|---|---|---|
| Calories | .......120 | Sugars .........3g |
| Protein | ........15g | Fat ...........3g |
| Carbohydrate | ....8g | Saturates ......1g |

5 MINS    40 MINS

### SERVES 4

## INGREDIENTS

25 g/1 oz rolled oats

1 tbsp chopped fresh rosemary

4 skinless chicken quarters

1 egg white

150 g/5½ oz natural low-fat fromage frais

2 tsp wholegrain mustard

salt and pepper

grated carrot salad, to serve

1 Mix together the rolled oats, chopped fresh rosemary and salt and pepper.

2 Brush each piece of chicken evenly with egg white, then coat in the oat mixture.

3 Place the chicken pieces on a baking tray and bake in a preheated oven, 200°C/400°F/Gas Mark 6, for about 40 minutes. Test to see if the chicken is cooked by inserting a skewer into the thickest part of the chicken – the juices should run clear without a trace of pink.

4 Mix together the fromage frais and mustard, season with salt and pepper to taste.

5 Serve the chicken, hot or cold, with the sauce and a grated carrot salad.

# Hot Pot Chops

A Hot Pot is a lamb casserole, made with carrots and onions and with a potato topping. The chops used here are an interesting alternative.

## NUTRITIONAL INFORMATION

Calories .......250  Sugars .........2g
Protein ........27g  Fat ..........12g
Carbohydrate ....8g  Saturates ......5g

10 MINS          30 MINS

### SERVES 4

## I N G R E D I E N T S

4 lean, boneless lamb leg steaks,
    about 125 g/4½ oz each

1 small onion, thinly sliced

1 medium carrot, thinly sliced

1 medium potato, thinly sliced

1 tsp olive oil

1 tsp dried rosemary

salt and pepper

fresh rosemary, to garnish

freshly steamed green vegetables,
    to serve

1 Preheat the oven to 180°C/350°F/Gas Mark 4. Using a sharp knife, trim any excess fat from the lamb steaks.

2 Season both sides of the steaks with salt and pepper and arrange them on a baking tray.

3 Alternate layers of sliced onion, carrot and potato on top of each lamb steak.

4 Brush the tops of the potato lightly with oil, season well with salt and pepper to taste and then sprinkle with a little dried rosemary.

5 Bake the hot pot chops in the oven for 25–30 minutes until the lamb is tender and cooked through.

6 Drain the lamb on absorbent kitchen paper (paper towels) and transfer to a warmed serving plate.

7 Garnish with fresh rosemary and serve accompanied with a selection of green vegetables.

## VARIATION

This recipe would work equally well with boneless chicken breasts. Pound the chicken slightly with a meat mallet or covered rolling pin so that the pieces are the same thickness throughout.

# Kibbeh

This Lebanese barbeque dish is similar to the Turkish kofte and the Indian kofta, but the spices used to flavour the meat are quite different.

## NUTRITIONAL INFORMATION

Calories . . . . . . .232    Sugars . . . . . . . . .3g
Protein . . . . . . . .19g   Fat . . . . . . . . . .13g
Carbohydrate . . . .9g    Saturates . . . . . .4g

1 HOUR          15 MINS

### SERVES 4

## I N G R E D I E N T S

75 g/2¾ oz couscous

1 small onion

350 g/12 oz lean minced lamb

½ tsp ground cinnamon

¼ tsp cayenne

4 tsp ground allspice

green salad and onion rings, to serve

### B A S T E

2 tbsp tomato ketchup

2 tbsp sunflower oil

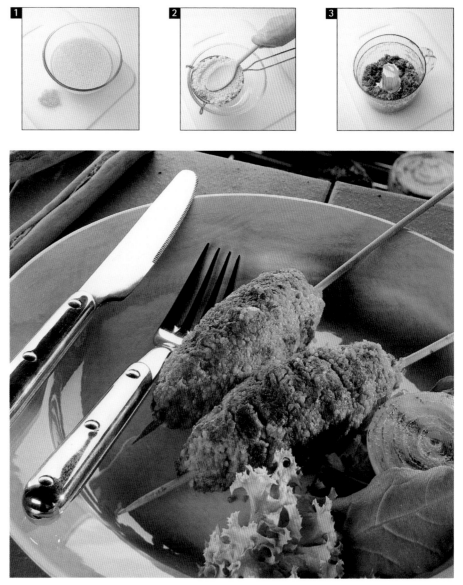

1 Place the couscous in a large bowl, cover with cold water and leave to stand for 30 minutes or until the couscous has swelled and softened. Alternatively, soak the couscous according to the instructions on the packet.

2 Drain the couscous through a sieve and squeeze out as much moisture as you can.

3 If you have a food processor, add the onion and chop finely. Add the lamb and process briefly to chop the mince further. If you do not have a processor, grate the onion then add to the lamb.

4 Combine the couscous, lamb and spices and mix well together. Divide the mixture into 8 equal sized portions. Press and shape the mixture around 8 skewers, pressing the mixture together firmly so that it holds it shape. Leave to chill for at least 30 minutes or until required.

5 To make the baste, combine the oil and ketchup.

6 Barbecue the kibbeh over hot coals for 10–15 minutes, turning and basting frequently. Serve with barbecued onion rings and green salad leaves.

# Lamb with a Spice Crust

Lamb neck fillet is a tender cut that is not too thick and is, therefore, ideal for cooking on the barbecue.

## NUTRITIONAL INFORMATION

Calories . . . . . . .203    Sugars . . . . . . . . .9g
Protein . . . . . . . .16g    Fat . . . . . . . . . .10g
Carbohydrate . . .12g    Saturates . . . . . .4g

5 MINS          45 MINS

### SERVES 4

## INGREDIENTS

1 tbsp olive oil

2 tbsp light muscovado sugar

2 tbsp wholegrain mustard

1 tbsp horseradish sauce

1 tbsp plain flour

350 g/12 oz neck fillet of lamb

salt and pepper

### TO SERVE

coleslaw

slices of tomato

1 Combine the oil, sugar, mustard, horseradish sauce, flour and salt and pepper to taste in a shallow, non-metallic dish until they are well mixed.

2 Roll the lamb in the spice mixture until well coated.

3 Lightly oil one or two pieces of foil or a large, double thickness of foil. Place the lamb on the foil and wrap it up so that the meat is completely enclosed.

4 Place the foil parcel over hot coals for 30 minutes, turning the parcel over occasionally.

5 Open the kitchen foil, spoon the cooking juices over the lamb and continue to barbecue for a further 10-15 minutes or until cooked through.

6 Placer the lamb on a platter and remove the foil. Cut into thick slices and serve with coleslaw and tomato slices.

## COOK'S TIP

If preferred, the lamb can be completely removed from the kitchen foil for the second part of the cooking. Barbecue the lamb directly over the coals for a smokier barbecue flavour, basting with extra oil if necessary.

# Pork & Apple Skewers

Flavoured with mustard and served with a mustard sauce, these kebabs make an ideal lunch.

**NUTRITIONAL INFORMATION**

| | |
|---|---|
| Calories .......290 | Sugars ........11g |
| Protein ........24g | Fat ..........17g |
| Carbohydrate ....11g | Saturates ......5g |

10 MINS 15 MINS

**SERVES 4**

## INGREDIENTS

450 g/1 lb pork fillet

2 eating apples

a little lemon juice

1 lemon

2 tsp wholegrain mustard

2 tsp Dijon mustard

2 tbsp apple or orange juice

2 tbsp sunflower oil

crusty brown bread, to serve

### MUSTARD SAUCE

1 tbsp wholegrain mustard

1 tsp Dijon mustard

6 tbsp single cream

1 To make the mustard sauce, combine the wholegrain and Dijon mustards in a small bowl and slowly blend in the cream. Leave to stand until required.

2 Cut the pork fillet into bite-size pieces and set aside until required.

3 Core the apples, then cut them into thick wedges. Toss the apple wedges in a little lemon juice – this will prevent any discoloration. Slice the lemon.

4 Thread the pork, apple and lemon slices alternately on to 4 metal or pre-soaked wooden skewers.

5 Mix together the mustards, apple or orange juice and sunflower oil. Brush the mixture over the kebabs and barbecue over hot coals for 10–15 minutes, until cooked through, frequently turning and basting the kebabs with the mustard marinade.

6 Transfer the kebabs to warm serving plates and spoon over a little of the mustard sauce. Serve the kebabs with fresh, crusty brown bread.

# Ginger Beef with Chilli

Serve these fruity, hot and spicy steaks with noodles. Use a non-stick ridged frying pan to cook with a minimum of fat.

## NUTRITIONAL INFORMATION

Calories .......179  Sugars .........8g
Protein ........21g  Fat ...........6g
Carbohydrate ....8g  Saturates ......2g

40 MINS     10 MINS

### SERVES 4

## INGREDIENTS

4 lean beef steaks (such as rump,
  sirloin or fillet), 100 g/3½ oz each

2 tbsp ginger wine

2.5 cm/1 inch piece root ginger,
  finely chopped

1 garlic clove, crushed

1 tsp ground chilli

1 tsp vegetable oil

salt and pepper

red chilli strips, to garnish

### TO SERVE

freshly cooked noodles

2 spring onions, shredded

### RELISH

225 g/8 oz fresh pineapple

1 small red pepper

1 red chilli

2 tbsp light soy sauce

1 piece stem ginger in syrup,
  drained and chopped

1 Trim any excess fat from the beef if necessary. Using a meat mallet or covered rolling pin, pound the steaks until 1 cm/½ inch thick. Season on both sides and place in a shallow dish.

2 Mix the ginger wine, root ginger, garlic and chilli and pour over the meat. Cover and chill for 30 minutes.

3 Meanwhile, make the relish. Peel and finely chop the pineapple and place it in a bowl. Halve, deseed and finely chop the pepper and chilli. Stir into the pineapple together with the soy sauce and stem ginger. Cover and chill until required.

4 Brush a grill pan with the oil and heat until very hot. Drain the beef and add to the pan, pressing down to seal. Lower the heat and cook for 5 minutes. Turn the steaks over and cook for a further 5 minutes.

5 Drain the steaks on kitchen paper and transfer to serving plates. Garnish with chilli strips, and serve with noodles, spring onions and the relish.

# Meatball Brochettes

Children will love these tasty meatballs on a skewer, which are economical and easy to make on the barbecue.

## NUTRITIONAL INFORMATION

Calories . . . . . . .120　Sugars . . . . . . . . .2g
Protein . . . . . . . .17g　Fat . . . . . . . . . .5g
Carbohydrate . . . .2g　Saturates . . . . . .2g

1 HOUR      10 MINS

### SERVES 4

## I N G R E D I E N T S

25 g/1 oz cracked wheat

350 g/12 oz lean minced beef

1 onion, chopped very finely (optional)

1 tbsp tomato ketchup

1 tbsp brown fruity sauce

1 tbsp chopped, fresh parsley

beaten egg, to bind

8 cherry tomatoes

8 button mushrooms

oil, to baste

8 bread finger rolls, to serve

1 Place the cracked wheat in a bowl and cover with boiling water. Leave to soak for 20 minutes or until softened. Drain thoroughly and leave to cool.

2 Place the soaked wheat, minced beef, onion, ketchup, brown fruity sauce and chopped fresh parsley together in a mixing bowl and mix well until all the ingredients are well combined. Add a little beaten egg if necessary to bind the mixture together.

3 Using your hands, shape the meat mixture into 18 even-sized balls. Leave to chill in the refrigerator for 30 minutes.

4 Thread the meatballs on to 8 pre-soaked wooden skewers, alternating them with the cherry tomatoes and button mushrooms.

5 Brush the brochettes with a little oil and barbecue over hot coals for about 10 minutes, until cooked through, turning occasionally and brushing with a little more oil if the meat starts to dry out.

6 Transfer the meatball brochettes to warm serving plates. Cut open the bread finger rolls and push the meat and vegetables off the skewer into the open rolls, using a fork. Serve immediately.

# Pork with Ratatouille Sauce

Serve this delicious combination of meat and vegetables with baked potatoes for an appetizing supper dish.

## NUTRITIONAL INFORMATION

Calories . . . . . . .230      Sugars . . . . . . . . .8g
Protein . . . . . . . .29g     Fat . . . . . . . . . . .9g
Carbohydrate . . . .8g         Saturates . . . . . .3g

🄶 10 MINS        🕐 35 MINS

### SERVES 4

## INGREDIENTS

4 lean, boneless pork chops,
   about 125 g/4½ oz each

1 tsp dried mixed herbs

salt and pepper

baked potatoes, to serve

### SAUCE

1 medium onion

1 garlic clove

1 small green pepper, deseeded

1 small yellow pepper, deseeded

1 medium courgette, trimmed

100 g/3½ oz button mushrooms

400 g/14 oz can chopped tomatoes

2 tbsp tomato purée

1 tsp dried mixed herbs

1 tsp caster sugar

## COOK'S TIP

This vegetable sauce could
be served with any other grilled
or baked meat or fish. It would
also make an excellent alternative
filling for savoury crêpes.

1 To make the sauce, peel and chop the onion and garlic. Dice the peppers. Dice the courgette. Wipe and halve the mushrooms.

2 Place all of the vegetables in a saucepan and stir in the chopped tomatoes and tomato purée. Add the dried herbs, sugar and plenty of seasoning. Bring to the boil, cover and simmer for 20 minutes.

3 Meanwhile, preheat the grill to medium. Trim away any excess fat from the chops, then season on both sides and rub in the dried mixed herbs. Cook the chops for 5 minutes, then turn over and cook for a further 6–7 minutes or until cooked through.

4 Drain the chops on absorbent kitchen paper and serve accompanied with the sauce and baked potatoes.

# Sweet Lamb Fillet

Lamb fillet, enhanced by a sweet and spicy glaze, is cooked on the barbecue in a kitchen foil parcel for deliciously moist results.

## NUTRITIONAL INFORMATION

Calories .......258  Sugars ........13g
Protein ........24g  Fat ..........13g
Carbohydrate ...13g  Saturates ......5g

5 MINS      1 HOUR

### SERVES 4

## INGREDIENTS

2 fillets of neck of lean lamb,
    each 225 g/8 oz

1 tbsp olive oil

½ onion, chopped finely

1 clove garlic, crushed

2.5 cm/1 inch piece root ginger, grated

5 tbsp apple juice

3 tbsp smooth apple sauce

1 tbsp light muscovado sugar

1 tbsp tomato ketchup

½ tsp mild mustard

salt and pepper

green salad leaves, croûtons and fresh
    crusty bread, to serve

1 Place the lamb fillet on a large piece of double thickness kitchen foil. Season with salt and pepper to taste.

2 Heat the oil in a small pan and fry the onion and garlic for 2–3 minutes until softened but not browned. Stir in the grated ginger and cook for 1 minute, stirring occasionally.

3 Stir in the apple juice, apple sauce, sugar, ketchup and mustard and bring to the boil. Boil rapidly for about 10 minutes until reduced by half. Stir the mixture occasionally so that it does not burn and stick to the base of the pan.

4 Brush half of the sauce over the lamb, then wrap up the lamb in the kitchen foil to completely enclose it. Barbecue the lamb parcels over hot coals for about 25 minutes, turning the parcel over occasionally.

5 Open out the kitchen foil and brush the lamb with some of the sauce. Continue to barbecue for a further 15–20 minutes or until cooked through.

6 Place the lamb on a chopping board, remove the foil and cut into thick slices. Transfer to serving plates and spoon over the remaining sauce. Serve with green salad leaves, croûtons and fresh crusty bread.

# Tangy Pork Fillet

Barbecued in a parcel of kitchen foil, these tasty pork fillets are served with a tangy orange sauce.

### NUTRITIONAL INFORMATION

| | | |
|---|---|---|
| Calories | .......230 | Sugars ........16g |
| Protein | ........19g | Fat ...........9g |
| Carbohydrate | ...20g | Saturates ......3g |

10 MINS    55 MINS

**SERVES 4**

## INGREDIENTS

400 g/14 oz lean pork fillet

3 tbsp orange marmalade

grated rind and juice of 1 orange

1 tbsp white wine vinegar

dash of Tabasco sauce

salt and pepper

### SAUCE

1 tbsp olive oil

1 small onion, chopped

1 small green pepper, deseeded and
    thinly sliced

1 tbsp cornflour

150 ml/5 fl oz orange juice

### TO SERVE

cooked rice

mixed salad leaves

1 Place a large piece of double thickness foil in a shallow dish. Put the pork fillet in the centre of the foil and season.

2 Heat the marmalade, orange rind and juice, vinegar and Tabasco sauce in a small pan, stirring until the marmalade melts and the ingredients combine. Pour the mixture over the pork and wrap the meat in foil, making sure that the parcel is well sealed so that the juices cannot run

out. Place over hot coals and barbecue for about 25 minutes, turning the parcel occasionally.

3 For the sauce, heat the oil and cook the onion for 2–3 minutes. Add the pepper and cook for 3–4 minutes.

4 Remove the pork from the kitchen foil and place on to the rack. Pour the juices into the pan with the sauce.

5 Barbecue the pork for a further 10–20 minutes, turning, until cooked through and golden on the outside.

6 In a small bowl, mix the cornflour with a little orange juice to form a paste. Add to the sauce with the remaining cooking juices. Cook, stirring, until the sauce thickens. Slice the pork, spoon over the sauce and serve with rice and mixed salad leaves.

# Teppanyaki

This simple, Japanese style of cooking, is ideal for thinly-sliced breast of chicken. You can use thin turkey escalopes, if you prefer.

## NUTRITIONAL INFORMATION

| | | |
|---|---|---|
| Calories .......206 | Sugars .........4g | |
| Protein ........30g | Fat ..........7g | |
| Carbohydrate ....6g | Saturates ......2g | |

5 MINS    10 MINS

**SERVES 4**

## I N G R E D I E N T S

4 boneless chicken breasts

1 red pepper

1 green pepper

4 spring onions

8 baby corn cobs

100 g/3½ oz bean sprouts

1 tbsp sesame or sunflower oil

4 tbsp soy sauce

4 tbsp mirin

1 tbsp grated fresh ginger root

1 Remove the skin from the chicken and slice at a slight angle, to a thickness of about 5 mm/¼ inch.

2 Deseed and thinly slice the peppers and trim and slice the spring onions and corn cobs.

3 Arrange the peppers, spring onions, corn and bean sprouts on a plate with the sliced chicken.

4 Heat a large griddle or heavy frying pan then lightly brush with oil. Add the vegetables and chicken slices in small batches, allowing space between them so that they cook thoroughly.

5 Combine the soy sauce, mirin and ginger and serve as a dip with the chicken and vegetables.

## COOK'S TIP

Mirin is a rich, sweet rice wine which you can buy in oriental shops, but if it is not available add 1 tablespoon of soft light brown sugar to the sauce instead.

# Karahi Chicken

A karahi is an extremely versatile two-handled metal pan, similar to a wok. Food is always cooked over a high heat in a karahi.

## NUTRITIONAL INFORMATION

| | |
|---|---|
| Calories . . . . . . . .270 | Sugars . . . . . . . . .1g |
| Protein . . . . . . . .41g | Fat . . . . . . . . . . .11g |
| Carbohydrate . . . .1g | Saturates . . . . . .2g |

5 MINS    20 MINS

SERVES 4

## INGREDIENTS

2 tbsp ghee

3 garlic cloves, crushed

1 onion, chopped finely

2 tbsp garam masala

1 tsp coriander seeds, ground

½ tsp dried mint

1 bay leaf

750 g/1 lb 10 oz lean boneless chicken meat, diced

200 ml/7 fl oz chicken stock

1 tbsp fresh coriander, chopped

salt

warm naan bread or chapatis, to serve

1 Heat the ghee in a karahi, wok or a large, heavy frying pan. Add the garlic and onion. Stir-fry for about 4 minutes until the onion is golden.

2 Stir in the garam masala, ground coriander, mint and bay leaf.

3 Add the chicken and cook over a high heat, stirring occasionally, for about 5 minutes. Add the stock and simmer for 10 minutes, until the sauce has thickened and the chicken juices run clear when the meat is tested with a sharp knife.

4 Stir in the fresh coriander and salt to taste, mix well and serve immediately with warm naan bread or chapatis.

## COOK'S TIP

Always heat a karahi or wok before you add the oil to help maintain the high temperature.

# Lime Chicken Kebabs

These succulent chicken kebabs are coated in a sweet lime dressing and are served with a lime and mango relish. They make an ideal light meal.

## NUTRITIONAL INFORMATION

| | | |
|---|---|---|
| Calories .......199 | Sugars ........14g | |
| Protein ........28g | Fat ..........4g | |
| Carbohydrate ...14g | Saturates ......1g | |

15 MINS     10 MINS

### SERVES 4

## INGREDIENTS

4 lean boneless chicken breasts, skinned, about 125 g/4½ oz each

3 tbsp lime marmalade

1 tsp white wine vinegar

½ tsp lime rind, finely grated

1 tbsp lime juice

salt and pepper

### TO SERVE

lime wedges

boiled white rice, sprinkled with chilli powder

### SALSA

1 small mango

1 small red onion

1 tbsp lime juice

1 tbsp fresh coriander, chopped

## COOK'S TIP

To prevent sticking, lightly oil metal skewers or dip bamboo skewers in water before threading the chicken on to them.

1 Slice the chicken breasts into thin pieces and thread on to 8 skewers so that the meat forms an S-shape down each skewer.

2 Preheat the grill to medium. Arrange the chicken kebabs on the grill rack. Mix together the lime marmalade, vinegar, lime rind and juice. Season with salt and pepper to taste. Brush the dressing generously over the chicken and grill for 5 minutes. Turn the chicken over, brush with the dressing again and grill for a further 4–5 minutes until the chicken is cooked through.

3 Meanwhile, prepare the salsa. Peel the mango and slice the flesh off the smooth, central stone. Dice the flesh into small pieces and place in a small bowl.

4 Peel and finely chop the onion and mix into the mango, together with the lime juice and chopped coriander. Season, cover and chill until required.

5 Serve the chicken kebabs with the salsa, accompanied with wedges of lime and boiled rice sprinkled with chilli powder.

# Cajun Chicken Gumbo

This complete main course is cooked in one saucepan. If you're cooking for one, halve the ingredients – the cooking time should stay the same.

## NUTRITIONAL INFORMATION

Calories .......425  Sugars .........8g
Protein ........34g  Fat ..........12g
Carbohydrate ...48g  Saturates ......3g

5 MINS          25 MINS

### SERVES 2

## INGREDIENTS

1 tbsp sunflower oil

4 chicken thighs

1 small onion, diced

2 sticks celery, diced

1 small green pepper, diced

90 g/3 oz long grain rice

300 ml/½ pint chicken stock

1 small red chilli

225 g/8 oz okra

15 ml/1 tbsp tomato purée

salt and pepper

1 Heat the oil in a wide pan and fry the chicken until golden. Remove the chicken from the pan.

2 Stir in the onion, celery and pepper and fry for 1 minute. Pour off any excess oil.

3 Add the rice and fry, stirring for a further minute. Add the stock and heat until boiling. Thinly slice the chilli and trim the okra. Add to the pan with the tomato purée. Season to taste.

4 Return the chicken to the pan and stir. Cover tightly and simmer gently for 15 minutes, or until the rice is tender, the chicken is thoroughly cooked and the liquid absorbed. Stir occasionally and if it becomes too dry, add a little extra stock.

## COOK'S TIP

The whole chilli makes the dish hot and spicy – if you prefer a milder flavour, discard the seeds of the chilli.

# Citrus Duckling Skewers

The tartness of citrus fruit goes well with the rich meat of duckling.
Duckling makes a change from chicken for the barbecue.

## NUTRITIONAL INFORMATION

| | | |
|---|---|---|
| Calories .......205 | Sugars .........5g | |
| Protein ........24g | Fat ..........10g | |
| Carbohydrate ....5g | Saturates ......2g | |

45 MINS    20 MINS

### SERVES 12

## INGREDIENTS

3 duckling breasts, skinned, boned and cut
  into bite-size pieces

1 small red onion, cut into wedges

1 small aubergine, cut into cubes

lime and lemon wedges, to garnish
  (optional)

### MARINADE

grated rind and juice of 1 lemon

grated rind and juice of 1 lime

grated rind and juice of 1 orange

1 clove garlic, crushed

1 tsp dried oregano

2 tbsp olive oil

dash of Tabasco sauce

1 Cut the duckling into bite-sized pieces. Place in a non-metallic bowl together with the prepared vegetables.

2 To make the marinade, place the lemon, lime and orange rinds and juices, garlic, oregano, oil and Tabasco sauce in a screw-top jar and shake until well combined. Pour the marinade over the duckling and vegetables and toss to coat. Leave to marinate for 30 minutes.

3 Remove the duckling and vegetables from the marinade and thread them on to skewers, reserving the marinade.

4 Barbecue the skewers on an oiled rack over medium hot coals, turning and basting frequently with the reserved marinade, for 15-20 minutes until the meat is cooked through. Serve the kebabs garnished with lemon and lime wedges for squeezing (if using).

## COOK'S TIP

For more zing add 1 teaspoon of chilli sauce to the marinade. The meat can be marinated for several hours, but it is best to marinate the vegetables separately for only about 30 minutes.

# Ginger Chicken & Corn

Chicken wings and corn in a sticky ginger marinade are designed to be eaten with the fingers – there's no other way!

## NUTRITIONAL INFORMATION

| | | | |
|---|---|---|---|
| Calories | .......123 | Sugars | .........3g |
| Protein | ........14g | Fat | ...........6g |
| Carbohydrate | ....3g | Saturates | ......1g |

🍖 10 MINS  🕐 20 MINS

### SERVES 6

## INGREDIENTS

3 cobs fresh sweetcorn

12 chicken wings

2.5 cm/1 inch piece fresh ginger root

6 tbsp lemon juice

4 tsp sunflower oil

1 tbsp golden caster sugar

jacket potatoes or salad, to serve

1 Remove the husks and silks from the corn. Using a sharp knife, cut each cob into 6 slices.

2 Place the corn in a large bowl with the chicken wings.

3 Peel and grate the ginger root or chop finely. Place in a bowl and add the lemon juice, sunflower oil and golden caster sugar. Mix together until well combined.

4 Toss the corn and chicken in the ginger mixture to coat evely.

5 Thread the corn and chicken wings alternately on to metal or pre-soaked wooden skewers, to make turning easier.

6 Cook under a preheated moderately hot grill or barbecue for 15–20 minutes, basting with the gingery glaze and turning frequently until the corn is golden brown and tender and the chicken is cooked. Serve with jacket potatoes or salad.

## COOK'S TIP

Cut off the wing tips before grilling as they burn very easily. Alternatively, you can cover them with small pieces of foil.

# Mexican Chicken

Chilli, tomatoes and corn are typical ingredients in a Mexican dish.
This is a quick and easy meal for unexpected guests.

## NUTRITIONAL INFORMATION

| | |
|---|---|
| Calories . . . . . . . .207 | Sugars . . . . . . . .8g |
| Protein . . . . . . . .18g | Fat . . . . . . . . . . .9g |
| Carbohydrate . . .13g | Saturates . . . . . .2g |

5 MINS      35 MINS

### SERVES 4

## I N G R E D I E N T S

2 tbsp oil

8 chicken drumsticks

1 medium onion, finely chopped

1 tsp chilli powder

1 tsp ground coriander

425 g/15 oz can chopped tomatoes

2 tbsp tomato purée

125 g/4½ oz frozen sweetcorn

salt and pepper

### TO SERVE

boiled rice

mixed pepper salad

1 Heat the oil in a large frying pan, add the chicken drumsticks and cook over a medium heat until lightly browned on all sides. Remove from the pan and set aside.

2 Add the onion to the pan and cook for 3–4 minutes until soft, then stir in the chilli powder and coriander and cook for a few seconds.

3 Add the chopped tomatoes with their juice and the tomato purée.

4 Return the chicken to the pan and simmer gently for 20 minutes until the chicken is tender and thoroughly cooked. Add the sweetcorn and cook a further 3–4 minutes. Season to taste.

5 Serve with boiled rice and mixed pepper salad.

## COOK'S TIP

If you dislike the heat of the chillies, just leave them out – the chicken will still taste delicious.

# Prawn Bhuna

This is a fiery recipe with subtle undertones. As the flavour of the prawns should be noticeable, the spices should not take over.

## NUTRITIONAL INFORMATION

Calories . . . . . . . .141  Sugars . . . . . . .0.4g

Protein . . . . . . . .19g  Fat . . . . . . . . . .7g

Carbohydrate . . . .1g  Saturates . . . . . .1g

15 MINS  20 MINS

### SERVES 4–6

## I N G R E D I E N T S

2 dried red chillies, deseeded if liked

3 fresh green chillies, finely chopped

1 tsp ground turmeric

3 garlic cloves, crushed

½ tsp pepper

1 tsp paprika

2 tsp white wine vinegar

½ tsp salt

500 g/1 lb 2 oz uncooked peeled
  king prawns

3 tbsp oil

1 onion, chopped very finely

175 ml/6 fl oz water

2 tbsp lemon juice

2 tsp garam masala

sprigs of fresh coriander, to garnish

## COOK'S TIP

Garam masala should be used sparingly and is generally added to foods towards the end of their cooking time. It is also used sprinkled over cooked meats, vegetables and pulses as a garnish.

1 Combine the chillies, spices, vinegar and salt in a non-metallic bowl. Stir in the prawns and leave for 10 minutes.

2 Heat the oil in a large frying pan or wok, add the onion and fry for 3–4 minutes until soft.

3 Add the prawns and the contents of the bowl to the pan and stir-fry over a high heat for 2 minutes. Reduce the heat, add the water and boil for 10 minutes, stirring occasionally, until the water is evaporated and the curry is fragrant.

4 Stir in the lemon juice and garam masala then transfer the mixture to a warm serving dish and garnish with fresh coriander sprigs.

5 Serve garnished with sprigs of fresh coriander.

# Salmon Yakitori

The Japanese sauce used here combines well with salmon, although it is usually served with chicken.

## NUTRITIONAL INFORMATION

| | | |
|---|---|---|
| Calories . . . . . . . .247 | Sugars . . . . . . . .10g | |
| Protein . . . . . . . .19g | Fat . . . . . . . . . . .11g | |
| Carbohydrate . . .12g | Saturates . . . . . .2g | |

20 MINS     15 MINS

### SERVES 4

## I N G R E D I E N T S

350 g/12 oz chunky salmon fillet

8 baby leeks

### Y A K I T O R I   S A U C E

5 tbsp light soy sauce

5 tbsp fish stock

2 tbsp caster sugar

5 tbsp dry white wine

3 tbsp sweet sherry

1 clove garlic, crushed

1 Skin the salmon and cut the flesh into 5 cm/2 inch chunks. Trim the leeks and cut them into 5 cm/2 inch lengths.

2 Thread the salmon and leeks alternately on to 8 pre-soaked wooden skewers. Leave to chill in the refrigerator until required.

3 To make the sauce, place all of the ingredients in a small pan and heat gently, stirring, until the sugar has dissolved.

4 Bring to the boil, then reduce the heat and simmer for 2 minutes. Strain the sauce through a fine sieve and leave to cool until it is required.

5 Pour about one-third of the sauce into a small dish and set aside to serve with the kebabs.

6 Brush plenty of the remaining sauce over the skewers and cook directly on the rack.

7 If preferred, place a sheet of oiled kitchen foil on the rack and cook the salmon on that.

8 Barbecue the salmon and leek kebabs over hot coals for about 10 minutes or until cooked though, turning once.

9 Use a brush to baste frequently during cooking with the remaining sauce in order to prevent the fish and vegetables from drying out. Transfer the kebabs to a large serving platter and serve with a small bowl of the reserved sauce for dipping.

# Baked Sea Bass

Sea bass is often paired with subtle oriental flavours. For a special occasion, you may like to bone the fish.

## NUTRITIONAL INFORMATION

Calories .......140    Sugars .......0.1g
Protein ........29g    Fat ...........1g
Carbohydrate ...0.1g   Saturates .....0.2g

🕙 10 MINS      🕐 15 MINS

### SERVES 4–6

## I N G R E D I E N T S

2 sea bass, about 1 kg/2 lb 4 oz each,
  cleaned and scaled

2 spring onions, green part only,
  cut into strips

5 cm/2 inch piece ginger, peeled and cut
  into strips

2 garlic cloves, unpeeled, crushed lightly

2 tbsp mirin or dry sherry

salt and pepper

### TO SERVE

pickled sushi ginger

soy sauce

1 For each fish lay out a double thickness of foil and oil the top piece well, or lay a piece of silicon paper over the foil.

2 Place the fish in the middle and expose the cavity.

3 Divide the spring onion and ginger between each cavity. Put a garlic clove in each cavity.

4 Pour over the mirin or dry sherry. Season the fish well.

5 Close the cavities and lay each fish on its side. Bring over the foil and fold the edges together to seal securely. Fold each end neatly.

6 Cook over a medium barbecue for 15 minutes, turning once.

7 To serve, remove the foil and cut each fish into 2 or 3 pieces.

8 Serve with the pickled ginger (if using) accompanied by soy sauce.

### COOK'S TIP

Fresh sea bass is just as delicious when cooked very simply. Stuff the fish with garlic and chopped herbs, brush with olive oil and bake in the oven.

# Curried Crab

If you can buy fresh crab, clean the shell and brush lightly with oil and use as a container for the crab meat.

## NUTRITIONAL INFORMATION

Calories . . . . . . .272   Sugars . . . . . . . . .5g
Protein . . . . . . . .27g   Fat . . . . . . . . . .16g
Carbohydrate . . . .5g   Saturates . . . . . .2g

5 MINS          15 MINS

### SERVES 4

## I N G R E D I E N T S

2 tbsp mustard oil

1 tbsp ghee

1 onion, chopped finely

5 cm/2 inch piece ginger root, grated

2 garlic cloves, peeled but left whole

1 tsp ground turmeric

1 tsp salt

1 tsp chilli powder

2 fresh green chillies, chopped

1 tsp paprika

125 g/4½ oz brown crab meat

350 g/12 oz white crab meat

250 ml/9 fl oz low-fat natural yogurt

1 tsp garam masala

basmati rice, to serve

fresh coriander, to garnish

1 Heat the mustard oil in a large, preferably non-stick, frying pan, wok or saucepan.

2 When it starts to smoke, add the ghee and onion. Stir for 3 minutes over a medium heat until the onion is soft.

3 Stir in the ginger and whole garlic cloves.

4 Add the turmeric, salt, chilli powder, chillies and paprika. Mix thoroughly.

5 Increase the heat and add the crab meat and yogurt. Simmer, stirring occasionally, for 10 minutes until the sauce is thickened slightly.

6 Add garam masala to taste.

7 Serve hot, over plain basmati rice, with the fresh coriander either chopped or in sprigs.

## COOK'S TIP

For an unusual combination of flavours, mix the crab meat with segments of grapefruit in a mayonnaise. Sprinkle with slivers of almonds.

# Lemony Monkfish Skewers

A simple basting sauce is brushed over these tasty kebabs. When served with crusty bread, they make a perfect light meal.

## NUTRITIONAL INFORMATION

| | |
|---|---|
| Calories . . . . . . . . .191 | Sugars . . . . . . . . .2g |
| Protein . . . . . . . .21g | Fat . . . . . . . . . . .11g |
| Carbohydrate . . . .1g | Saturates . . . . . .1g |

10 MINS     15 MINS

### SERVES 4

## I N G R E D I E N T S

450 g/1 lb monkfish tail

2 courgettes

1 lemon

12 cherry tomatoes

8 bay leaves

### S A U C E

3 tbsp olive oil

2 tbsp lemon juice

1 tsp chopped, fresh thyme

½ tsp lemon pepper

salt

### T O  S E R V E

green salad leaves

fresh, crusty bread

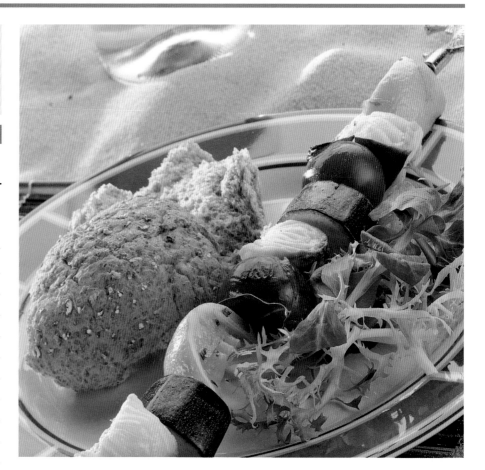

1 Cut the monkfish into 5 cm/2 inch chunks.

## VARIATION

Use plaice fillets instead of the monkfish, if you prefer. Allow two fillets per person, and skin and cut each fillet lengthways into two. Roll up each piece and thread them on to the skewers.

2 Cut the courgettes into thick slices and the lemon into wedges.

3 Thread the monkfish, courgettes, lemon, tomatoes and bay leaves on to 4 skewers.

4 To make the basting sauce, combine the oil, lemon juice, thyme, lemon pepper and salt to taste in a small bowl.

5 Brush the basting sauce liberally all over the fish, lemon, tomatoes and bay leaves on the skewers.

6 Cook the skewers on the barbecue for about 15 minutes over medium-hot coals, basting them frequently with the sauce, until the fish is cooked through. Transfer the skewers to plates and serve with green salad leaves and wedges of crusty bread.

# Fragrant Tuna Steaks

Fresh tuna steaks are very meaty – they have a firm texture, yet the flesh is succulent. Steaks from the belly are best of all.

## NUTRITIONAL INFORMATION

| | | | |
|---|---|---|---|
| Calories | .......239 | Sugars | .......0.1g |
| Protein | ........42g | Fat | ...........8g |
| Carbohydrate | ...0.5g | Saturates | ......2g |

15 MINS          15 MINS

### SERVES 4

## INGREDIENTS

4 tuna steaks, 175 g/6 oz each

½ tsp finely grated lime rind

1 garlic clove, crushed

2 tsp olive oil

1 tsp ground cumin

1 tsp ground coriander

pepper

1 tbsp lime juice

fresh coriander, to garnish

### TO SERVE

avocado relish (see Cook's Tip, below)

lime wedges

tomato wedges

## COOK'S TIP

For the avocado relish, peel and chop a small ripe avocado. Mix in 1 tbsp lime juice, 1 tbsp freshly chopped coriander, 1 small finely chopped red onion and some chopped fresh mango or tomato. Season to taste.

1 Trim the skin from the tuna steaks, rinse and pat dry on absorbent kitchen paper.

2 In a small bowl, mix together the lime rind, garlic, olive oil, cumin, ground coriander and pepper to make a paste.

3 Spread the paste thinly on both sides of the tuna. Heat a non-stick, ridged frying pan until hot and press the tuna steaks into the pan to seal them. Lower the heat and cook for 5 minutes. Turn the fish over and cook for a further 4–5 minutes until the fish is cooked through. Drain on kitchen paper and transfer to a serving plate.

4 Sprinkle the lime juice and chopped coriander over the fish. Serve with avocado relish (see Cook's Tip), and tomato and lime wedges.

# Char-Grilled Mackerel

The sharpness of the apricot glaze complements the oiliness of the fish and has a delicious hint of ginger.

## NUTRITIONAL INFORMATION

| | | | |
|---|---|---|---|
| Calories | .......343 | Sugars | ........21g |
| Protein | ........23g | Fat | ..........18g |
| Carbohydrate | ...22g | Saturates | ......4g |

5 MINS      10 MINS

### SERVES 4

## INGREDIENTS

4 mackerel, about 225 g/8 oz each

400 g/14 oz can apricots in natural juice

3 tbsp dark muscovado sugar

3 tbsp Worcestershire sauce

3 tbsp soy sauce

2 tbsp tomato purée

1 tsp ground ginger

dash Tabasco sauce

1 clove garlic, crushed (optional)

salt and pepper

1 Clean and gut the mackerel, removing the heads if preferred. Place the fish in a shallow dish.

2 Drain the apricots, reserving the juice. Roughly chop half of the apricots and set aside. Place the remaining apricots in a food processor with the sugar, Worcestershire sauce, soy sauce, tomato purée, ginger, Tabasco sauce and garlic (if using) and process until smooth. Alternatively, chop the apricots and mix with the other ingredients. Season to taste.

3 Pour the sauce over the fish, turning them so that they are well coated on both sides. Leave to chill in the refrigerator until required.

4 Transfer the mackerel to the barbecue either directly on the rack or on a piece of greased kitchen foil. Barbecue the mackerel over hot coals for 5–7 minutes, turning once.

5 Spoon any remaining marinade into a saucepan. Add the reserved chopped apricots and about half of the reserved apricot juice and bring to the boil. Reduce the heat and simmer for 2 minutes. Transfer the mackerel to a serving plate and serve with the apricot sauce.

## COOK'S TIP

Use a hinged rack if you have one as it will make it much easier to turn the fish during barbecueing.

# Scallop Skewers

As the scallops are marinated, it is not essential that they are fresh; frozen shellfish are fine for a barbecue.

## NUTRITIONAL INFORMATION

| | |
|---|---|
| Calories .......182 | Sugars .........0g |
| Protein ........29g | Fat ...........7g |
| Carbohydrate ....0g | Saturates ......1g |

30 MINS   10 MINS

SERVES 4

## INGREDIENTS

grated zest and juice of 2 limes

2 tbsp finely chopped lemon grass or 1 tbsp lemon juice

2 garlic cloves, crushed

1 green chilli, deseeded and chopped

16 scallops, with corals

2 limes, each cut into 8 segments

2 tbsp sunflower oil

1 tbsp lemon juice

salt and pepper

### TO SERVE

60 g/2 oz rocket salad

200 g/7 oz mixed salad leaves

1 Soak 8 skewers in warm water for at least 10 minutes before you use them to prevent the food from sticking.

2 Combine the lime juice and zest, lemon grass, garlic and chilli together in a pestle and mortar or spice grinder to make a paste.

3 Thread 2 scallops on to each of the soaked skewers. Cover the ends with foil to prevent them from burning.

4 Alternate the scallops with the lime segments.

5 Whisk together the oil, lemon juice, salt and pepper to make the dressing.

6 Coat the scallops with the spice paste and place over a medium barbecue, basting occasionally.

7 Cook for 10 minutes, turning once.

8 Toss the rocket, mixed salad leaves and dressing together well. Put into a serving bowl.

9 Serve the scallops piping hot, 2 skewers on each plate, with the salad.

# Green Fish Curry

This dish has a wonderful fresh, hot, exotic taste resulting from the generous amount of fresh herbs, sharp fresh chillies and coconut milk.

### NUTRITIONAL INFORMATION

| | | | |
|---|---|---|---|
| Calories | .......223 | Sugars | .........2g |
| Protein | ........44g | Fat | ..........5g |
| Carbohydrate | ....2g | Saturates | ......1g |

🍳 5 MINS    🕐 20 MINS

**SERVES 4**

## INGREDIENTS

1 tbsp oil

2 spring onions, sliced

1 tsp cumin seeds, ground

2 fresh green chillies, chopped

1 tsp coriander seeds, ground

4 tbsp chopped fresh coriander

4 tbsp chopped fresh mint

1 tbsp chopped chives

150 ml/¼ pint coconut milk

4 white fish fillets, about 225 g/8 oz each

salt and pepper

basmati rice, to serve

1 mint sprig, to garnish

1 Heat the oil in a large frying pan or shallow saucepan and add the spring onions.

2 Stir-fry the spring onions over a medium heat until they are softened but not coloured.

3 Stir in the cumin, chillies and ground coriander, and cook until fragrant.

4 Add the fresh coriander, mint, chives and coconut milk and season liberally.

5 Carefully place the fish in the pan and poach for 10–15 minutes until the flesh flakes when tested with a fork.

6 Serve the fish fillets in the sauce with the rice. Garnish with a mint sprig.

## COOK'S TIP

Never overcook fish – it is surprising how little time it takes compared to meat. It will continue to cook slightly while keeping warm in the oven and while being dished up and brought to the table.

# Plaice with Mushrooms

The moist texture of grilled fish is complemented by the texture of the mushrooms.

## NUTRITIONAL INFORMATION

| | | |
|---|---|---|
| Calories . . . . . . . .243 | Sugars . . . . . . . . .2g |
| Protein . . . . . . . .30g | Fat . . . . . . . . . .13g |
| Carbohydrate . . . .2g | Saturates . . . . . .3g |

10 MINS          20 MINS

### SERVES 4

## I N G R E D I E N T S

4 × 150 g/5½ oz white-skinned plaice fillets

2 tbsp lime juice

celery salt and pepper

90 g/3 oz low-fat spread

300 g/10½ oz mixed small mushrooms such as button, oyster, shiitake, chanterelle or morel, sliced or quartered

4 tomatoes, skinned, seeded and chopped

basil leaves, to garnish

mixed salad, to serve

1 Line a grill rack with baking parchment and place the fish on top.

2 Sprinkle over the lime juice and season with celery salt and pepper.

3 Place under a preheated moderate grill and cook for 7–8 minutes without turning, until just cooked. Keep warm.

4 Meanwhile, gently melt the low fat spread in a non-stick frying pan, add the mushrooms and fry for 4–5 minutes over a low heat until cooked through.

5 Gently heat the tomatoes in a small saucepan.

6 Spoon the mushrooms, with any pan juices, and the tomatoes over the plaice.

7 Garnish the grilled plaice with the basil leaves and serve with a mixed salad.

## COOK'S TIP

Mushrooms are ideal in a low-fat diet, as they are packed full of flavour and contain no fat. More 'meaty' types of mushroom, such as chestnut, will take slightly longer to cook.

# Fish with Black Bean Sauce

Any firm and delicate fish steaks such as salmon or salmon trout can be cooked by the same method.

## NUTRITIONAL INFORMATION

| | | | |
|---|---|---|---|
| Calories | .......194 | Sugars | .......0.2g |
| Protein | ........27g | Fat | ...........9g |
| Carbohydrate | ....1g | Saturates | ......1g |

5 MINS      20 MINS

### SERVES 6

## I N G R E D I E N T S

1 sea bass, trout or turbot, weighing about 700g/1 lb 9 oz, cleaned

1 tsp salt

1 tbsp sesame oil

2-3 spring onions, cut in half lengthways

1 tbsp light soy sauce

1 tbsp Chinese rice wine or dry sherry

1 tbsp finely shredded ginger root

1 tbsp oil

2 tbsp crushed black bean sauce

2 finely shredded spring onions

fresh coriander leaves, to garnish (optional)

lemon slices, to garnish

1 Score both sides of the fish with diagonal cuts at 2.5 cm/1 inch intervals. Rub both the inside and outside of the fish with salt and sesame oil.

2 Place the fish on top of the spring onions on a heat-proof platter. Blend the soy sauce and wine with the ginger shreds and pour evenly all over the fish.

3 Place the fish on the platter in a very hot steamer (or inside a wok on a rack), cover and steam vigorously for 12-15 minutes.

4 Heat the oil until hot, then blend in the black bean sauce. Remove the fish from the steamer and place on a serving dish.

5 Pour the hot black bean sauce over the whole length of the fish and place the shredded spring onions on top. Place the fish on a platter and serve garnished with coriander leaves (if using) and lemon slices.

## COOK'S TIP

If using fish steaks, rub them with the salt and sesame oil, but do not score with a knife. The fish may require less cooking, depending on the thickness of the steaks – test with a skewer after about 8 minutes to check whether they are done.

# Scallops with Mushrooms

Scallops have a rich but delicate flavour. When sautéed with mushrooms and bathed in brandy and cream, they make a really special meal.

## NUTRITIONAL INFORMATION

| | | | |
|---|---|---|---|
| Calories | .......390 | Sugars | .........1g |
| Protein | ........31g | Fat | ..........28g |
| Carbohydrate | ....1g | Saturates | ......4g |

5 MINS    10 MINS

### SERVES 2

## I N G R E D I E N T S

15 g/½ oz butter

225 g/8 oz shelled queen scallops

1 tbsp olive oil

50 g/1¾ oz oyster mushrooms, sliced

50 g/1¾ oz shiitake mushrooms, sliced

1 garlic clove, chopped

4 spring onions, white and green
    parts sliced

3 tbsp double cream

1 tbsp brandy

salt and pepper

sprigs of fresh dill, to garnish

basmati rice to serve

1 Heat the butter in a heavy-based frying pan and fry the scallops for about 1 minute, turning occasionally.

2 Remove the scallops from the frying pan with a perforated spoon and keep warm.

3 Add the olive oil to the pan and heat. Add the mushrooms, garlic and spring onions and cook for 2 minutes, stirring constantly.

4 Return the scallops to the pan. Add the double cream and brandy, stirring well to mix.

5 Season with salt and pepper to taste and heat to warm through.

6 Garnish with fresh dill sprigs and serve with rice.

### COOK'S TIP

Scallops, which consist of a large, round white muscle with bright orange roe, are the most delicious seafood in the prettiest of shells. The rounded half of the shell can be used as a dish in which to serve the scallops.

# Baked Trout Mexican-Style

Make this dish as hot or as mild as you like by adjusting the amount of red chilli. The green chillies are milder and add a pungency to the dish.

## NUTRITIONAL INFORMATION

| | |
|---|---|
| Calories .......329 | Sugars .........5g |
| Protein ........53g | Fat ..........10g |
| Carbohydrate ....6g | Saturates ......2g |

10 MINS     30 MINS

### SERVES 4

## INGREDIENTS

4 trout, 225 g/8 oz each

1 small bunch fresh coriander

4 shallots, shredded finely

1 small yellow pepper, deseeded and very finely chopped

1 small red pepper, deseeded and very finely chopped

2 green chillies, deseeded and finely chopped

1–2 red chillies, deseeded and finely chopped

1 tbsp lemon juice

1 tbsp white wine vinegar

2 tsp caster sugar

salt and pepper

fresh coriander, to garnish

salad leaves, to serve

## COOK'S TIP

For the chilli bean rice, cook 225 g/8 oz long-grain white rice. Drain and rinse a 400 g/14 oz can kidney beans and stir into the rice with 1 tsp each of ground cumin and coriander. Stir in 4 tbsp chopped fresh coriander and season.

1 Preheat the oven to 180°C/350°F/ Gas Mark 4. Wash the trout and pat dry with kitchen paper. Season and stuff with coriander leaves.

2 Place the fish side by side in a shallow ovenproof dish. Sprinkle over the shallots, peppers and chillies.

3 Mix together the lemon juice, vinegar and sugar in a bowl. Spoon over the trout and season with salt and pepper. Cover the dish and bake for 30 minutes or until the fish is tender and the flesh is opaque.

4 Remove the the fish with a fish slice and drain. Transfer to warm serving plates and spoon the cooking juices over the fish. Garnish with fresh coriander and serve with salad and chilli bean rice (see Cook's Tip).

# Oriental Vegetable Noodles

This dish has a mild, nutty flavour from the peanut butter and dry-roasted peanuts.

## NUTRITIONAL INFORMATION

| | | | |
|---|---|---|---|
| Calories | .......193 | Sugars | .........5g |
| Protein | .........7g | Fat | ..........12g |
| Carbohydrate | ...14g | Saturates | ......2g |

10 MINS    15 MINS

### SERVES 4

## I N G R E D I E N T S

175 g/6 oz green thread noodles or
   multi-coloured spaghetti

1 tsp sesame oil

2 tbsp crunchy peanut butter

2 tbsp light soy sauce

1 tbsp white wine vinegar

1 tsp clear honey

125 g/4½ oz daikon, grated

125 g/4½ oz/1 large carrot, grated

125 g/4½ oz cucumber, shredded finely

1 bunch spring onions, shredded finely

1 tbsp dry-roasted peanuts, crushed

### TO GARNISH

carrot flowers

spring onion tassels

1 Bring a large saucepan of water to the boil, add the noodles or spaghetti and cook according to the packet instructions. Drain well and rinse in cold water. Leave in a bowl of cold water until required.

2 To make the peanut butter sauce, put the sesame oil, peanut butter, soy sauce, vinegar, honey and seasoning into a small screw-top jar. Seal and shake well to mix thoroughly.

3 Drain the noodles or spaghetti well, place in a large serving bowl and mix in half the peanut sauce.

4 Using 2 forks, toss in the daikon, carrot, cucumber and spring onions. Sprinkle with crushed peanuts and garnish with carrot flowers and spring onion tassels. Serve the noodles with the remaining peanut sauce.

### COOK'S TIP

There are many varieties of oriental noodles available from oriental markets, delicatessens and supermarkets. Try rice noodles, which contain very little fat and require little cooking; usually soaking in boiling water is sufficient.

# Char-Grilled Vegetables

This medley of peppers, courgettes, aubergine and red onion can be served on its own or as an unusual side dish.

## NUTRITIONAL INFORMATION

| | | |
|---|---|---|
| Calories ........66 | Sugars .........7g | |
| Protein .........2g | Fat ...........3g | |
| Carbohydrate ....7g | Saturates .....0.5g | |

15 MINS    15 MINS

### SERVES 4

## INGREDIENTS

1 large red pepper

1 large green pepper

1 large orange pepper

1 large courgette

4 baby aubergines

2 medium red onions

2 tbsp lemon juice

1 tbsp olive oil

1 garlic clove, crushed

1 tbsp chopped, fresh rosemary or 1 tsp dried rosemary

salt and pepper

### TO SERVE

cracked wheat, cooked

tomato and olive relish

1 Halve and deseed the peppers and cut into even sized pieces, about 2.5 cm/ 1 inch wide.

2 Trim the courgettes, cut in half lengthways and slice into 2.5 cm/ 1 inch pieces. Place the peppers and courgettes in a large bowl.

3 Trim the aubergines and quarter them lengthways. Peel both the onions, then cut each one into 8 even-sized wedges.

4 Add the pieces of aubergine and onions to the bowl containing the wedges of peppers and courgettes.

5 In a small bowl, whisk together the lemon juice, olive oil, garlic, rosemary and seasoning.

6 Pour the mixture over the vegetables and stir to coat evenly.

7 Preheat the grill to medium. Thread the vegetables on to 8 metal or pre-soaked wooden skewers. Arrange the kebabs on the rack and cook for 10–12 minutes, turning frequently until the vegetables are lightly charred and just softened.

8 Drain the vegetable kebabs and serve on a bed of cracked wheat accompanied with a tomato and olive relish.

# Spinach & Orange Salad

This is a refreshing and very nutritious salad. Add the dressing just before serving so that the leaves do not become soggy.

## NUTRITIONAL INFORMATION

Calories .......126  Sugars ........10g
Protein .........3g  Fat ..........9g
Carbohydrate ...10g  Saturates ......1g

10 MINS     0 MINS

SERVES 4

## INGREDIENTS

225 g/8 oz baby spinach leaves

2 large oranges

½ red onion

### DRESSING

3 tbsp extra virgin olive oil

2 tbsp freshly squeezed orange juice

2 tsp lemon juice

1 tsp clear honey

½ tsp wholegrain mustard

salt and pepper

1 Wash the spinach leaves under cold running water and then dry them thoroughly on absorbent kitchen paper. Remove any tough stalks and tear the larger leaves into smaller pieces.

2 Slice the top and bottom off each orange with a sharp knife, then remove the peel. Carefully slice between the membranes of the orange to remove the segments. Reserve any juices for the salad dressing.

3 Using a sharp knife, finely chop the onion.

4 Mix together the salad leaves and orange segments and arrange in a serving dish.

5 Scatter the chopped onion over the salad.

6 To make the dressing, whisk together the olive oil, orange juice, lemon juice, honey, mustard and salt and pepper to taste in a small bowl.

7 Pour the dressing over the salad just before serving. Toss the salad well to coat the leaves with the dressing.

**VARIATION**
Use a mixture of spinach and watercress leaves, if you prefer a slightly more peppery flavour.

# Coronation Salad

This dish is based on Coronation Chicken which was invented to celebrate Queen Victoria's coronation as a symbol of Anglo-Indian links.

## NUTRITIONAL INFORMATION

| | | | |
|---|---|---|---|
| Calories | .......236 | Sugars | ........24g |
| Protein | .........7g | Fat | ..........5g |
| Carbohydrate | ...43g | Saturates | ......1g |

25 MINS    0 MINS

### SERVES 4

## INGREDIENTS

1 red pepper

60 g/2 oz sultanas

1 celery stick, sliced

125 g/4½ oz sweetcorn

1 Granny Smith apple, diced

125 g/4½ oz white seedless grapes, washed and halved

250 g/9 oz cooked basmati rice

60 g/2 oz/½ cup cooked, peeled prawns (optional)

1 cos lettuce, washed and drained

1 tsp paprika to garnish

### DRESSING

4 tbsp low-fat mayonnaise

2 tsp mild curry powder

1 tsp lemon juice

1 tsp paprika

pinch of salt

1 Deseed and chop the red pepper.

2 Combine the sultanas, red pepper, celery, sweetcorn, apple and grapes in a large bowl. Stir in the rice, and prawns, if using.

3 For the dressing, put the mayonnaise, curry powder, lemon juice, paprika and salt into a small bowl and mix well.

4 Pour the dressing over the salad and gently mix until evenly coated.

5 Line the serving plate with cos lettuce leaves and spoon on the salad. Sprinkle over the paprika and serve.

### COOK'S TIP

Mayonnaise can be bought in varying thicknesses, from the type that you spoon out of the jar to the pouring variety. If you need to thin down mayonnaise for a dressing, simply add water little by little until the desired consistency is reached.

# Minted Fennel Salad

This is a very refreshing salad. The subtle liquorice flavour of fennel combines well with the cucumber and mint.

## NUTRITIONAL INFORMATION

Calories . . . . . . . .90  Sugars . . . . . . . . .7g
Protein . . . . . . . . .4g  Fat . . . . . . . . . . .5g
Carbohydrate . . . .7g  Saturates . . . . . . .1g

25 MINS        0 MINS

### SERVES 4

## I N G R E D I E N T S

1 bulb fennel

2 small oranges

1 small or ½ large cucumber

1 tbsp chopped mint

1 tbsp virgin olive oil

2 eggs, hard boiled

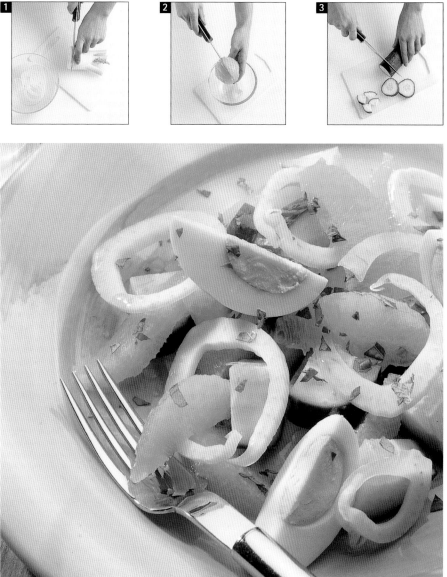

1 Using a sharp knife, trim the outer leaves from the fennel. Slice the fennel bulb thinly into a bowl of water and then sprinkle with lemon juice (see Cook's Tip).

2 Grate the rind of the oranges over a bowl. Using a sharp knife, pare away the orange peel, then segment the orange by carefully slicing between each line of pith. Do this over the bowl in order to retain the juice.

3 Using a sharp knife, cut the cucumber into 12 mm/½ inch rounds and then cut each round into quarters.

4 Add the cucumber to the fennel and orange mixture together with the mint.

5 Pour the olive oil over the fennel and cucumber salad and toss well.

6 Peel and quarter the eggs and use these to decorate the top of the salad. Serve at once.

### COOK'S TIP

Fennel will discolour if it is left for any length of time without a dressing. To prevent any discoloration, place it in a bowl of water and sprinkle with lemon juice.

# Moroccan Couscous Salad

Couscous is a type of semolina made from durum wheat. It is wonderful in salads as it readily takes up the flavour of the dressing.

## NUTRITIONAL INFORMATION

Calories .......195  Sugars ........15g
Protein .........8g  Fat ...........2g
Carbohydrate ...40g  Saturates .....0.3g

15 MINS      15 MINS

### SERVES 6

## INGREDIENTS

2 cups couscous

1 bunch spring onions, trimmed and chopped finely

1 small green pepper, cored, deseeded, and chopped

10 cm/4 inch piece cucumber, chopped

200 g/7 oz can chickpeas, rinsed and drained

⅔ cup sultanas

2 oranges

salt and pepper

lettuce leaves, to serve

sprigs of fresh mint, to garnish

### DRESSING

finely grated rind of 1 orange

1 tbsp chopped fresh mint

⅔ cup low-fat natural yogurt

1 Put the couscous into a bowl and cover with boiling water. Leave it to soak for about 15 minutes to swell the grains, then stir with a fork to separate them.

2 Add the spring onions, green pepper, cucumber, chickpeas and sultanas to the couscous, stirring to combine. Season well with salt and pepper.

3 To make the dressing, mix the orange rind, mint, and yogurt. Pour over the couscous mixture and stir well.

4 Using a sharp serrated knife, remove the peel and pith from the oranges. Cut the flesh into segments, removing all the membrane.

5 Arrange the lettuce leaves on serving plates. Divide the couscous mixture between the plates and arrange the orange segments on top.

6 Garnish with sprigs of fresh mint and serve.

## VARIATION

As an alternative, use bulgar wheat instead of the couscous. Rinse thoroughly until the water runs clear, then soak in boiling water for 1 hour. Sieve if necessary.

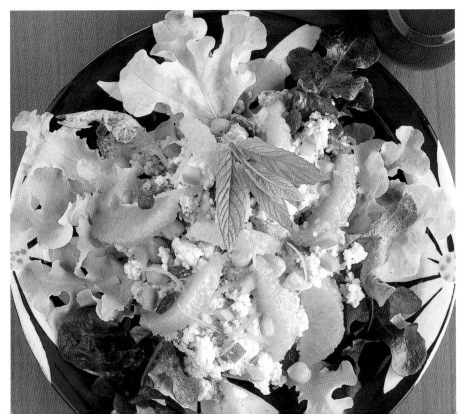

# Mussel Salad

A colourful combination of cooked mussels tossed together with char-grilled red peppers and salad leaves in a lemon dressing.

## NUTRITIONAL INFORMATION

| | | |
|---|---|---|
| Calories | ....... 124 | Sugars ......... 5g |
| Protein | ........ 16g | Fat ........... 5g |
| Carbohydrate | .... 5g | Saturates ...... 1g |

40 MINS    10 MINS

**SERVES 4**

## INGREDIENTS

2 large red peppers

350 g/12 oz cooked shelled mussels, thawed if frozen

1 head of radicchio

25 g/1 oz rocket leaves

8 cooked New Zealand mussels in their shells

### TO SERVE

lemon wedges

crusty bread

### DRESSING

1 tbsp olive oil

1 tbsp lemon juice

1 tsp finely grated lemon rind

2 tsp clear honey

1 tsp French mustard

1 tbsp snipped fresh chives

salt and pepper

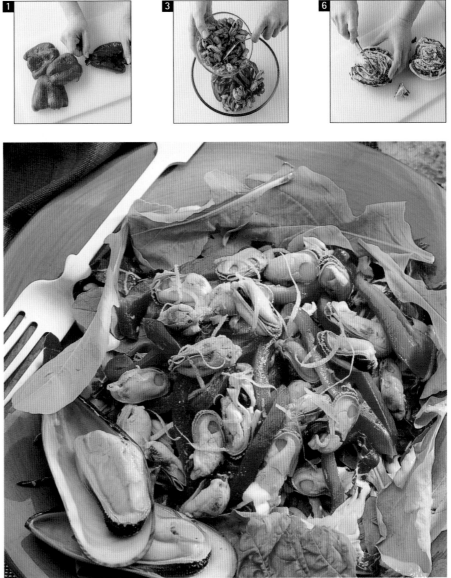

1 Preheat the grill to hot. Halve and deseed the peppers and place them skin-side up on the rack.

2 Cook for 8–10 minutes until the skin is charred and blistered and the flesh is soft. Leave to cool for 10 minutes, then peel off the skin.

3 Slice the pepper flesh into thin strips and place in a bowl. Gently mix in the shelled mussels and set aside until required.

4 To make the dressing, mix all of the ingredients until well blended.

5 Mix into the pepper and mussel mixture until coated.

6 Remove the central core of the radicchio and shred the leaves. Place in a serving bowl with the rocket leaves and toss together.

7 Pile the mussel mixture into the centre of the leaves and arrange the large mussels in their shells around the edge of the dish. Serve with lemon wedges and crusty bread.

# Sweet & Sour Fruit

This mixture of fresh and canned fruit, which has a sweet and sour flavour, is very cooling, especially in the summer.

## NUTRITIONAL INFORMATION

| | |
|---|---|
| Calories .......240 | Sugars ........58g |
| Protein .........2g | Fat ..........0.4g |
| Carbohydrate ...60g | Saturates ......0g |

5 MINS          0 MINS

### SERVES 4

## INGREDIENTS

400 g/14 oz can mixed fruit cocktail

400 g/14 oz can guavas

2 large bananas

3 apples (optional)

1 tsp ground black pepper

1 tsp salt

½ tsp ground ginger

2 tbsp lemon juice

fresh mint leaves, to garnish

1 Drain the can of mixed fruit cocktail and place the fruit in a deep mixing bowl.

2 Mix the the drained fruit cocktail wth the guavas and their syrup so that the fruit is well coated.

3 Peel the bananas and cut into thick slices.

4 Peel the apples (optional) and cut into dice.

5 Add the fresh fruit to the bowl containing the canned fruit and mix together.

6 Add the ground black pepper, salt and ginger and stir to mix. Add the lemon juice to prevent the banana and apple from turning brown and mix again.

7 Serve the sweet and sour fruit as a snack garnished with a few fresh mint leaves.

### COOK'S TIP

Guavas are tropical fruits with a powerful, exotic smell. You may find fresh guavas in specialist shops and large supermarkets, but the canned variety is more widely available. Surprisingly, they have a higher vitamin C content than many citrus fruits.

# Carrot & Orange Salad

A crunchy and colourful, sweet and savoury dish which would also make an excellent appetiser.

## NUTRITIONAL INFORMATION

Calories . . . . . . .194  Sugars . . . . . . . .25g
Protein . . . . . . . . .6g  Fat . . . . . . . . . . .8g
Carbohydrate . . .26g  Saturates . . . . . .1g

20 MINS        0 MINS

### SERVES 4

## I N G R E D I E N T S

500 g/1 lb 2 oz celeriac

2 tbsp orange juice

350 g/12 oz/4 carrots, sliced finely

2 celery sticks, chopped finely

25 g/1 oz celery leaves

4 oranges

25 g/1 oz walnut pieces

## D R E S S I N G

1 tbsp walnut oil

½ tsp grated orange rind

3 tbsp orange juice

1 tbsp white wine vinegar

1 tsp clear honey

salt and pepper

1 Trim and peel the celeriac and slice or grate finely into a bowl. Add the orange juice and toss together.

2 Mix in the carrots, celery and celery leaves. Cover and chill while preparing the oranges.

3 Slice off the tops and bottoms from the oranges. Using a sharp knife, slice off the skin, taking the pith away at the same time. Cut out the orange flesh by slicing along the side of the membranes dividing the segments. Gently mix the segments into the celeriac mixture.

4 To make the dressing, place all the ingredients in a small screw-top jar. Seal and shake well to mix.

5 Pile the vegetable mixture on to a plate. Sprinkle over the walnut pieces and serve with the dressing.

## COOK'S TIP

Celeriac is a variety of celery with a bulbous, knobbly root. It has a rough, light brown skin and creamy white flesh and is delicious raw or cooked.

# Tomato Salsa

This salad is used extensively in Mexican cooking and served as a dip or a relish, and is eaten as an accompaniment to almost any dish.

## NUTRITIONAL INFORMATION

| | |
|---|---|
| Calories . . . . . . . . .10 | Sugars . . . . . . . . .2g |
| Protein . . . . . . . .0.4g | Fat . . . . . . . . . .0.1g |
| Carbohydrate . . . .2g | Saturates . . . . . .0g |

🝰

🥘 10 MINS ⏱ 0 MINS

### SERVES 4

## I N G R E D I E N T S

4 ripe red tomatoes

1 medium red onion or 6 spring onions

1–2 garlic cloves, crushed (optional)

2 tbsp chopped fresh coriander

½ red or green chilli (optional)

finely grated rind of ½–1 lemon or lime

1–2 tbsp lemon or lime juice

pepper

1 Chop the tomatoes fairly finely and evenly, and put into a bowl. They must be firm and a good strong red colour for the best results, but if preferred, they may be peeled by placing them in boiling water for about 20 seconds and then plunging into cold water. The skins should then slip off easily when they are nicked with a knife.

2 Peel and slice the red onion thinly, or trim the spring onions and cut into thin slanting slices; add to the tomatoes with the garlic and coriander and mix lightly.

3 Remove the seeds from the red or green chilli (if using) chop the flesh very finely and add to the salad. Treat the chillies with care; do not touch your eyes or face after handling them until you have washed your hands thoroughly. Chilli juices can burn.

4 Add the lemon or lime rind and juice to the salsa, and mix well. Transfer to a serving bowl and sprinkle with pepper.

## COOK'S TIP

If you don't like the distinctive flavour of fresh coriander, you can replace it with flat-leaf parsley instead.

# Aubergine Curry

This is a rich vegetable dish, ideal served with a tandoori chicken and naan bread. It is also delicious served as a vegetarian dish with rice.

## NUTRITIONAL INFORMATION

Calories .......650  Sugars .........6g
Protein .........3g  Fat ...........4g
Carbohydrate ....6g  Saturates ......1g

15 MINS          15 MINS

### SERVES 6

## INGREDIENTS

2 whole aubergines

225 ml/8 fl oz low-fat natural yogurt

2 cardamom pods

½ tsp ground turmeric

1 dried red chilli

½ tsp coriander seeds

½ tsp ground black pepper

1 tsp garam masala

1 clove

2 tbsp sunflower oil

1 onion, sliced lengthways

2 garlic cloves, crushed

1 tbsp grated ginger root

6 ripe tomatoes, peeled, deseeded and quartered

fresh coriander, to garnish

1  If you have a gas cooker, roast the 2 aubergines over a naked flame, turning frequently, until charred and black all over  This should take about 5 minutes. Peel under running cold water. Cut off the stem end and discard.

2  Put the peeled aubergines into a large bowl and mash lightly with a fork. Stir in the yogurt.

3  Grind together the cardamom pods, turmeric, red chilli, coriander seeds, black pepper, garam masala and clove in a large pestle and mortar or spice grinder.

4  Heat the oil in a wok or heavy frying pan over a moderate heat and cook the onion, garlic and ginger root until soft. Add the tomatoes and ground spices, and stir well.

5  Add the aubergine mixture to the pan and stir well. Cook for 5 minutes over a gentle heat, stirring constantly, until all the flavours are combined, and some of the liquid has evaporated.

6  Serve the aubergine immediately, garnished with coriander.

# Sesame Seed Chutney

This chutney is delicious served with spiced rice dishes, and also makes an unusual filling to spread in sandwiches.

## NUTRITIONAL INFORMATION

| | | | |
|---|---|---|---|
| Calories | .......120 | Sugars | .........0g |
| Protein | .........4g | Fat | ..........12g |
| Carbohydrate | ...0.2g | Saturates | ......2g |

🕙 10 MINS  🕒 5 MINS

### SERVES 4

## I N G R E D I E N T S

8 tbsp sesame seeds

2 tbsp water

½ bunch fresh coriander

3 fresh green chillies, chopped

1 tsp salt

2 tsp lemon juice

chopped red chilli, to garnish

1 Place the sesame seeds in a large, heavy-based saucepan and dry roast them. Set the sesame seeds aside to cool.

2 Once cooled, place the sesame seeds in a food processor or pestle and mortar and grind well to form a fine powder.

3 Add the water to the sesame seeds and mix thoroughly to form a smooth paste.

4 Using a sharp knife, finely chop the coriander.

5 Add the chillies and coriander to the sesame seed paste and grind once again.

6 Add the salt and lemon juice to the mixture and grind once again.

7 Remove the mixture from the food processor or pestle and mortar and transfer to a serving dish. Garnish with red chilli and serve.

## COOK'S TIP

Dry roasting brings out the flavour of dried spices and takes just a few minutes. You will be able to tell when the spices are ready because of the wonderful fragrance that develops. Stir the spices constantly to ensure that they do not burn.

# Colcannon

This is an old Irish recipe, usually served with a piece of bacon, but it is equally delicious with chicken or fish.

## NUTRITIONAL INFORMATION

| | | | |
|---|---|---|---|
| Calories | . . . . . . . .102 | Sugars | . . . . . . . . .4g |
| Protein | . . . . . . . . .4g | Fat | . . . . . . . . . .4g |
| Carbohydrate | . . .14g | Saturates | . . . . .2g |

5 MINS     35 MINS

**SERVES 4**

# I N G R E D I E N T S

225 g/8 oz green cabbage, shredded

85 ml/3 fl oz skimmed milk

225 g/8 oz floury potatoes, diced

1 large leek, chopped

pinch of grated nutmeg

15 g/½ oz butter, melted

salt and pepper

1 Bring a large saucepan of salted water to the boil, add the shredded cabbage and cook for 7-10 minutes. Drain thoroughly and set aside.

2 Meanwhile, in a separate saucepan, bring the milk to the boil and add the potatoes and leek. Reduce the heat and simmer for 15-20 minutes or until they are cooked through.

## COOK'S TIP

There are many different varieties of cabbage, which produce hearts at varying times of year, so you can be sure of being able to make this delicious cabbage dish all year round.

3 Stir in the grated nutmeg and mash the potatoes and leeks together.

4 Add the drained cabbage to the potatoes and mix well.

5 Spoon the potato and cabbage mixture into a serving dish, making a

hollow in the centre with the back of a spoon.

6 Pour the melted butter into the hollow and serve the colcannon immediately.

# Chocolate & Pineapple Cake

Decorated with thick yogurt and canned pineapple, this is a low-fat cake, but it is by no means lacking in flavour.

## NUTRITIONAL INFORMATION

| | | | |
|---|---|---|---|
| Calories | .......199 | Sugars | ........19g |
| Protein | .........5g | Fat | ..........9g |
| Carbohydrate | ...28g | Saturates | ......3g |

10 MINS     25 MINS

### SERVES 9

## INGREDIENTS

150 g/5½ oz low-fat spread

125 g/4½ oz caster sugar

100 g/3½ oz self-raising flour, sieved

3 tbsp cocoa powder, sieved

1½ tsp baking powder

2 eggs

225g/8 oz can pineapple pieces in natural juice

125 ml/4 fl oz low-fat thick natural yogurt

about 1 tbsp icing sugar

grated chocolate, to decorate

1 Lightly grease a 20 cm/8 inch square cake tin.

2 Place the low-fat spread, caster sugar, flour, cocoa powder, baking powder and eggs in a large mixing bowl. Beat with a wooden spoon or electric hand whisk until smooth.

3 Pour the cake mixture into the prepared tin and level the surface. Bake in a preheated oven, 190°C/325°F/ Gas Mark 5, for 20-25 minutes or until

springy to the touch. Leave to cool slightly in the tin before transferring to a wire rack to cool completely.

4 Drain the pineapple, chop the pineapple pieces and drain again. Reserve a little pineapple for decoration, then stir the rest into the yogurt and sweeten to taste with icing sugar.

5 Spread the pineapple and yogurt mixture over the cake and decorate with the reserved pineapple pieces. Sprinkle with the grated chocolate.

# Tropical Fruit Fool

Fruit fools are always popular, and this light, tangy version will be no exception. Use your favourite fruits in this recipe if you prefer.

## NUTRITIONAL INFORMATION

Calories .......149  Sugars ........25g
Protein .........6g  Fat ..........0.4g
Carbohydrate ...32g  Saturates .....0.2g

35 MINS        0 MINS

### SERVES 4

## INGREDIENTS

1 medium ripe mango

2 kiwi fruit

1 medium banana

2 tbsp lime juice

½ tsp finely grated lime rind, plus extra to decorate

2 medium egg whites

425 g/15 oz can low-fat custard

½ tsp vanilla essence

2 passion fruit

1  To peel the mango, slice either side of the smooth, flat central stone. Roughly chop the flesh and blend the fruit in a food processor or blender until smooth. Alternatively, mash with a fork.

## VARIATION

Other tropical fruits to try include paw-paw purée, with chopped pineapple and dates or pomegranate seeds to decorate. Or make a summer fruit fool by using strawberry purée, topped with raspberries and blackberries and cherries.

2  Peel the kiwi fruit, chop the flesh into small pieces and place in a bowl. Peel and chop the banana and add to the bowl. Toss all of the fruit in the lime juice and rind and mix well.

3  In a grease-free bowl, whisk the egg whites until stiff and then gently fold in the custard and vanilla essence until thoroughly mixed.

4  In 4 tall glasses, alternately layer the chopped fruit, mango purée and custard mixture, finishing with the custard on top. Leave to chill in the refrigerator for 20 minutes.

5  Halve the passion fruits, scoop out the seeds and spoon the passion fruit over the fruit fools. Decorate each serving with the extra lime rind and serve.

This is a Parragon Book
This edition published in 2004

Parragon
Queen Street House
4 Queen Street
Bath BA1 1HE, UK

ISBN 1-40544-641-2

Printed in China

With grateful thanks to Claire Dashwood.

Notes
Use all metric or all imperial quantities, as the two are not interchangeable. Cup measurements in this book are for American cups. Tablespoons are assumed to be 15 ml. Unless otherwise stated, milk is assumed to be full fat, eggs are medium and pepper is freshly ground black pepper.

The nutritional information provided for each recipe is per serving or per portion. Optional ingredients, variations or serving suggestions have not been included in the calculations. The times given for each recipe are an approximate guide only as the preparation times may differ as a result of the type of oven used.